Emilio Iodice

THE COMMANDER IN CHIEF

The Qualities Needed of Leaders of Freedom-Loving
Nations in the 21st Century

**Lessons from
American Presidential
History**

**A Classic Guide for
Global Leadership**

The Oval Office, courtesy of White House Museum (http://www.whitehousemuseum.org/index.htm)

*Dedicated to my grandchildren,
those I love, and those who love me.*

Emilio Iodice

The Commander in Chief

The Qualities Needed of Leaders of Freedom-Loving
Nations in the 21st Century

**Lessons from
American Presidential
History**

**A Classic Guide for
Global Leadership**

ALSO BY EMILIO IODICE

Profiles in Leadership: From Caesar to Modern Times

A Kid from Philadelphia: Mario Lanza: The Voice of the Poet's Sisters

Future Shock 2.0, The Dragon Brief (a thriller about 2020, fiction based on fact)

Reflections: Stories of Love, Inspiration, Remembrance and Power

Electing the President, 2016, The Most Important Decision You Will Ever Make

When Courage Was the Essence of Leadership: Lessons from History

Coming soon: *Liberation: A World War II Thriller of Love, Compassion, Courage, Leadership and Redemption* (inspired by true stories)

Table of Contents

Emilio Iodice

PREFACE ━━━━━━━━━━━━━━━━━━━━━━━

As George Santayana so presciently admonished – and author Emilio Iodice reiterates – "If we do not learn from history, we are doomed to repeat it." Thus, knowing what has transpired in the past with respect to the inner workings of executive administrations, what leadership traits must be cherished and emulated, and which lessons learned are best to guide the way forward in both national and international governance, are all paramount in the selection of an American president. Conversely, erring in the choice of who inhabits the highest office in the land can have long-lasting, deleterious consequences. Thus, Iodice aids both constituent American and world watchers in examining American presidential history to identify the desired characteristics of a potential leader occupying such a multifaceted post.

In his analysis, Iodice explains the many roles a U.S. president occupies. The chief executive serves, *inter alia*, as commander-in-chief of the American armed forces, as head of the executive branch of a cross-checking democratic system, as top governmental administrator, as political party leader, and as global leader, stabilizer, and visionary. Furthermore, this quintessential leader is certainly not perfect, but, rather, continuously strives for perfection. S/he understands and welcomes critiques, refraining from reacting defensively to contrary analysis. It is the chief executive who is expected to form a vast, competent bureaucracy, tapping into the talent and skills of a diverse range of prospective advisors. As supplemental leaders, it is critical that these assistants attain their appointments strictly through a merit-based system.

America's imperfect past is well-demarcated by slavery, genocide of Native Americans, Jim Crow segregationist violence and inequities, disenfranchisement of women, and the dehumanization of communities of color. Even the U.S. Constitution was created by slaveowners and was itself an imperfect document, as repeatedly demonstrated by its many amendments and piecemeal judicial interpretations. In this manner, Iodice warns against unguarded reverence of foundational documents and the blind worship of past presidents and, quite frankly, all leaders in general. All leaders of utmost prominence must earn each constituent's trust and respect by exemplifying qualities. The genuine leader must actively engage with those they lead (Iodice cites Ronald Reagan's "Great Communicator" status and FDR's "Fireside Chats" as positive examples), as the greatness of a country is reflected by the respect generated by its president. The effective executive must live a moral life for the public to note and emulate. S/he must strive to be a reformer, creating and ensuring opportunities – such as, economic, career, housing – for the populace, while purging all elements of corruption and chastising public servants who shun their responsibilities.

Iodice clearly points out the significant power of younger generations to push for a bold, indefatigable leader who eschews racism and sexism and champions the causes important to these next generations – combatting climate change, promoting racial justice, and overhauling dark money in politics. The brashness, life experiences, integrity, and wisdom of Lincoln and the Roosevelts serve well as examples of such desired qualities – men who did not mask their individual limitations and committed firmly to promoting the public good. On the other hand, the corrupt, self-serving, and pandering business policies of a president such as Warren G. Harding strayed entirely from this servant focus.

In *Commander in Chief*, Iodice paints the quintessential leader as both a fair compromiser and unwavering collaborator. This individual must surround him/herself with the best and the brightest and work diligently across the political spectrum to avoid divisiveness and form a meaningful, enduring consensus. Those who have served successfully in the office of U.S. President have recognized their roles of stewards of the nation – as well as the world. For example, T. Roosevelt assumed the role of forger of America's national park system, highlighting the importance of nature's effect on all humankind, as well as the urgency to protect and cherish it. JFK opened space travel as the new frontier to be explored. Successful leaders have often ventured outside their respective comfort zones to address the inequities of the day–LBJ with the passage of both the Civil Rights Act of 1964 and the Voting Rights Act of 1965, and Lincoln with his tenacious work in effecting the passage of the 13th Amendment, are presented as prime examples of this highly regarded quality. These leaders never narrowed their duty to represent all constituents in lieu of merely protecting and pandering to a narrow, self-tailored support base. Another American president exhibiting this trait was Barack Obama, who said upon his inauguration in 2009 and repeatedly thereafter that he was the president of, and advocate for, ALL Americans. These revered public servants strive to tell the truth, engender public trustworthiness, demonstrate an unfailing commitment to honesty, and display unquestionable courage of character.

Iodice engages the reader in a narrative which compares past presidents, identifying the predominant characteristics of their respective administrations, placing the discussion within prescriptive historical context. For instance, he notes the oft-overlooked altruism of William McKinley as juxtaposed to the stark bloodthirstiness and ineptitude of Andrew Jackson. Rather, the truly effective, visionary leader takes full responsibility (in conformity with Harry Truman's "The buck stops here!" proclamation) and is accountable to all governed for his/her actions and policy choices. Further, this brand of leader displays one trait which has been notably absent in poorly run administrations – empathy. That leader implements the principles of the Golden Rule every day and in every public act by standing in the shoes of the marginalized, the hurt, and the forgotten. That leader embraces the promises of the future without being handcuffed by precedent. Failing to do so may, and has, cost countless lives and livelihoods.

The U.S. presidency is about making choices. It is about humility and humanism. In his examination of various presidential styles, Iodice calls on the reader to acknowledge the profound power of the voter to install a competent, well-respected leader. To achieve this objective, the voter must stay well-informed and correctly discern between factual reporting and fictional vitriol. Without so doing, all our lives, our fortunes, and our collective futures are in imminent danger. The American Experiment is put at risk. With such high stakes, Iodice presents us with an unequivocal call to arms – to establish a new coalition of conscience and to invoke our collective moral reckoning.

Prof. Elizabeth F. R. Gingerich, J.D.

Editor-in-Chief
The Louis S. and Mary L. Morgal Chair of Christian Business Ethics/ The W.A. Roper and Susan Morgal Vaughan Chair in Christian Business Ethics, Valparaiso University, Valparaiso, Indiana

INTRODUCTION

The desk of the President of the United States, termed the "Resolute Desk,"
courtesy of Jimmy Carter Library and Museum

The disinterested and effective work for decent politics depends on people who are willing at great personal inconvenience and sacrifice to give their time and money to the service of a cause, the triumph of which represents not one particle of advantage to themselves personally.

—Theodore Roosevelt, as quoted by the Raab Collection

Leaders determine our future and that of our children and grandchildren.

Leadership has never been more important than in the age of the Internet, which affects facts, ideas, feelings, and choices for all.

The experience of the United States in selecting a president is a guide for modern democracies and all people who want freedom.

We use the term, 'commander in chief,' to refer to or imply the broad powers of a nation's leader.

We examine the qualities that the head of state must have to succeed, not just as the leader of the military, but of wide-ranging roles that represents the country's spirit, traditions, ideals, and its inhabitants.

The history of the American presidency reveals traits and concepts relevant to any prime minister, head of a region, or governor of a state in any country that loves liberty and democracy.

The office of the President of the United States is more than an American institution. It embodies the feelings of the nation. It may be more important than the Congress or the Supreme Court, because it is the principal office that the public identifies with.

The president is the only official elected by all the people and is a symbolic leader who holds the hopes and dreams of the nation in his or her hands.

It is the closest we come to an American monarch.

In most democracies, the chief leader represents the aspirations of the nation, just as prime ministers express the desires of a people and symbolizes a country's ambitions and future.

Selecting the commander in chief is a matter of life or death, success or failure, peace or war, poverty or prosperity.

For this reason, those who seek this office must be held to a higher standard. They must have qualities we, as a people, insist upon. If not, we risk suffering chaos and turmoil as a nation.

History shows the significance of leadership for the destiny of a nation.

The decision of whom we put at the helm of our country must be made intelligently and carefully, and must be made by us, the voters.

Often, the electorate expresses frustration for the choices presented. A lack of participation in the political process creates this problem.

Leaders must be groomed, developed, and selected from the populace with primaries, local elections, and fair means of selection to prepare the best and the brightest for higher office. Without grass roots involvement in the search for political talent, a nation risks electing leaders who are not fit for office and only reflect specific interests and lobbies that are by no means for the public good.

Indifference is the enemy of self-determination.

Freedom is a right fought for against tyranny with blood.

Leaders must be defenders of liberty and be prepared to die on the altar of the republic to preserve it.

Partaking in the process of self-rule must begin at home and in school. Children must be taught that democracy seeks the greatest common benefit. Government by the people and for the people works to fulfill and protect human rights. It is the best method to resolve conflicts peacefully, avoid war, and allow individuals to use their talents for self-actualization in an atmosphere of autonomy, without fear of repression.

Leaders must be held accountable for their words, actions, and examples.

The responsibility is ours.

Blaming the media—which is supported by advertising to sell services and products to us, or powerful interests who depend on the public for their livelihood—shifts the burden to defend democracy to others.

Once we take on the onus to preserve our rights, everything changes.

In Shakespeare's *Julius Caesar*, Cassius said to his friend and co-conspirator in the murder of the dictator, "The fault, dear Brutus, is not in our stars, but in ourselves."

This work is a timeless look at American commanders in chief of the past. They show what leadership attributes we need today and tomorrow to govern. This is an ageless tool to help us choose intelligently and rationally, based on true history and true facts.

Our work is about the characteristics we should demand of leaders of freedom-loving nations who endeavor to provide opportunities for all in an atmosphere of justice and liberty.

A good leader should:[1]

- Have good character, first and foremost, which consists of honesty, ethics, courage, fortitude, loyalty, respect, a sense of responsibility, caring, and clear expressions of good citizenship.
- Strive for personal and professional growth through humility, empathy, and adversity.
- Exhibit self-confidence and surround themselves with talented, dedicated people.
- Work to motivate and inspire followers.
- Create a culture of respect for others and their opinions, ideas, and ideals.
- Take responsibility when things go wrong, and give others credit when all goes well.
- Avoid revenge and concentrating on past slights or wrongs.
- Develop direct connections with people and always be approachable and open to talk and listening to their views.
- Use stories to communicate and convey messages with the shared experiences of the time.
- Have strong emotional intelligence, control one's emotions, and avoid negative feelings.
- Have an innate curiosity and love of learning.
- Know how to relax and replenish their energy.
- Transform personal ambition into what is best for the greater good.

---

[1] Doris Kearns Goodwin (https://www.edsurge.com/news/2019-03-20-doris-kearns-goodwin-s-10-leadership-lessons-from-the-white-house)

No leader may have all the qualities we describe.

Regardless, we have a duty to select someone who comes as close to the ideal, without the illusion that saints sit in the Oval Office.

They do not.

At the same time, we cannot tolerate habitual sinners controlling the apparatus of the most powerful country on the planet.

The Achilles Heel of Leadership: The Human Dimension

This work is not complete without mentioning the current assessments of some of the people studied in this book.

Leaders are human beings.

Each has weaknesses and prejudices tempered by the time in which they live and the ideas and ideals they are taught.

"While never disregarding any historical figure's flaws, we should also remember that each generation of human beings depends on the cohorts that came before it for its religious and political institutions, its science and technology, and even for the very language it speaks. There is much to be gained from maintaining a balanced sense of respect and gratitude for the benefactions of our imperfect forebears."[2]

Even so, we need to be objective.

What is printed and what is held honorable about leaders is not always fact.

The sins of American presidents, looked at now, should make us think.

---

[2] "Sins of the Founding Fathers: The perils of judging past heroes by today's standards" (https://theconversation.com/sins-of-the-founding-fathers-the-perils-of-judging-past-heroes-by-todays-standards-46560)

Our values have changed. What is taking root is a better sense of fairness, justice, and equality, especially among young people. A movement is underway to examine our most important leaders of the past from the vantage point of today. We need to be honest in evaluating their faults, debating and condemning their acts, and not glorifying that part of their memory, especially when it represents prejudice, hatred, and measures taken against equality and justice.

Objectivity demands a 360-degree evaluation.

Recent examples are the cancellation of Jefferson and Jackson Day celebrations and the condemnation of Woodrow Wilson.

Thomas Jefferson and many of our founding fathers were slave owners. Andrew Jackson was responsible for the murder of thousands of Native Americans.

"Jefferson and his legacy have been one of the world's most influential forces for democracy, republican government, and the rights of the individual. In addition to his political contributions, Jefferson vigorously promoted the sciences and arts and founded the University of Virginia. And though Jefferson owned slaves and may have even fathered multiple children with a slave after his wife's death, he opposed it in his writings.

"In addition to founding the forerunner of today's Democratic Party, Jackson was a military hero who served two terms as the nation's seventh president, dismantled the national bank, overcame an effort by South Carolina to nullify federal law, secured Florida from the Spanish, and paid off the national debt. Of course, Jackson was also a slave owner and he forced Indian tribes from their lands, precipitating the so-called 'trail of tears.'"[3]

Woodrow Wilson was a racist.

---

[3] "Sins of the Founding Fathers: The perils of judging past heroes by today's standards" (https://theconversation.com/sins-of-the-founding-fathers-the-perils-of-judging-past-heroes-by-todays-standards-46560)

Introduction

Wilson overturned the great work of Theodore Roosevelt by removing African Americans from the U.S. Government who had earned their jobs through merit.

Wilson was considered a prominent head of Princeton University and a good governor of New Jersey.

As President, Wilson led the country into the Great War and established new parameters for peace in his Fourteen Points. He promoted the creation of the League of Nations.

"Though Wilson attended Princeton as an undergraduate, taught there and served from 1902 to 1910 as president, his name is to be removed from Princeton's School of Public and International Affairs. And why is this icon of American liberals to be so dishonored? Because Thomas Woodrow Wilson disbelieved in racial equality. Says Princeton President Christopher Eisgruber:

"'Wilson's racist opinions and policies make him an inappropriate namesake.' Moreover, Wilson's 'racism was significant and consequential, even by the standards of his own time.'" [4]

Racism can never be tolerated. America's "original sin" of slavery was criminal, in all senses of the word.

In a moving editorial in *The New York Times*, Caroline Randall Williams began her story this way:

"The black people I come from were owned and raped by the white people I come from. Who dares to tell me to celebrate them?"[5] She continues:

---

[4] (https://eu.app.com/story/opinion/columnists/2020/07/03/now-its-woodrow-wilsons-turn-where-does-end/3282942001/)

[5] "You Want a Confederate Monument? My Body Is a Confederate Monument" (https://www.google.com/search?client=firefox-b-d&q=You+Want+a+Confederate+Monument%3F+My+Body+Is+a+Confederate+Monument)

"But here is the thing: Our ancestors don't deserve your unconditional pride. Yes, I am proud of every one of my black ancestors who survived slavery. They earned that pride, by any decent person's reckoning. But I am not proud of my white ancestors, whom I know by virtue of my very existence, to be bad actors."[6]

No one can disagree.

At stake in the debate over the sins of our historic leaders is a larger concept. People in our era are easily labeled by one political persuasion or another, which often hides more than is revealed. But judging historical leaders in just a one-dimensional fashion oversimplifies their strengths, weaknesses, and leadership styles, and threatens to steal them of their humanity.

Character weaknesses deserve examination and condemnation, but they should not stop us from admiring the good acts and studying a nation's heroes, while also revealing their blemishes so we can view them from a full and complete point of view.[7]

---

[6] "You Want a Confederate Monument? My Body Is a Confederate Monument" (https://www.google.com/search?client=firefox-b-d&q=You+Want+a+Confederate+Monument%3F+My+Body+Is+a+Confederate+Monument)

[7] "Sins of the Founding Fathers: The perils of judging past heroes by today's standards" (https://theconversation.com/sins-of-the-founding-fathers-the-perils-of-judging-past-heroes-by-todays-standards-46560)

PART ONE: The American Presidency
CHAPTER ONE: ▬▬▬▬▬▬▬▬▬▬▬▬
Presidential Power

"To vastly improve your country and truly make it great again, start by choosing a better leader. Do not let the media or the establishment make you pick from the people they choose, but instead choose from those they do not pick."

— Suzy Kassem

No man who ever held the office of president would congratulate a friend on obtaining it."

— John Adams

Every four years, Americans elect a new Commander in Chief. The person chosen is not just President of the United States.

The position is of global leader, global decision maker, and global visionary, the most powerful leader on earth.

It demands reflection and care.

The Global Leader

Article II of the U.S. Constitution vests the executive power of the United States in the President, who is the Supreme Commander of American military forces around the world and is often referred to as the Commander in Chief.

In addition, the President has other essential responsibilities.

The Roles of the President of the United States

What are the roles of the President? The person selected must fulfill several complex and interconnected functions:[8]

- Chief of State: ceremonial head of the U.S.
- Chief Executive: holder of the executive power
- Chief Administrator: leader of the Executive branch of the Federal Government, responsible for enforcing the laws of the nation
- Chief Diplomat: main architect of American Foreign Policy and the nation's Chief Spokesperson to the world
- Commander in Chief: supreme leader of the nation's armed forces
- Chief Legislator: main author and architect of public policy
- Chief of Party: leader of his or her political party

KING ANDREW THE FIRST.

---

[8] Pearson, "The President's Job Description" (http://assets.pearsonschool.com/asset_mgr/legacy/200938/section1_jobdescription_26523_1.pdf)

In "*The Presidential Difference*," Fred I. Greenstein explained the role today:

> The power of modern American presidents manifests itself in its purest form in the global arena, where their actions as commander in chief can determine the fate of the human race. This was most strikingly evident in the extended nuclear standoff between the United States and the Soviet Union that followed World War II. However, the president's latitude for independent action is even greater in the unstructured post-cold war world than it was during the cold war, when the threat of mutual destruction concentrated minds and constrained actions.
>
> Presidential power is less potentially apocalyptic at home than abroad, but the occupant of the Oval Office is also of critical domestic importance. The power to nullify legislation gives the chief executive the capacity to thwart the will of Congress unless his veto is overridden by two-thirds of the Senate and House of Representatives. [9]
>
> The President has power of budget allocations and the execution of laws. He or she can sway public opinion and, even when facing impeachment, still retain their formal powers.
>
> All of this would lead one to expect the qualities that bear on a president's leadership to be subjected to the closest possible attention. That is far from the case. To be sure, every president has been the object of a deluge of prose, first during his presidency, then in the memoirs of his associates, and later in studies based on the declassified records of his administration. Yet, much of that outpouring is directed to the ends the president sought rather than the means he used to advance them, and a large portion of it bears on the merits of his policies rather than the attributes that shaped his leadership[10]

---

[9]. Fred I. Greenstein, *The Presidential Difference, Leadership Style From FDR to Clinton*, Free Press: New York, 2000, Chapter 1.
[10]. Greenstein, page 2

27President Roosevelt was accused of trying to "pack" the Supreme Court and add new members when the Court voted New Deal laws unconstitutional, February 8, 1937, courtesy of Chicago News, "What Did Uncle Vote For?"

"Checks and balances" were set up by the founders of the American republic as part of the US Constitution, to specify the functions and responsibilities of the President, the Congress, and the Supreme Court and to maintain a balance of power and "check" and limit each branch from becoming too influential. Since the beginning of the United States, the presidency has evolved, and more powers have been given to the president, especially in the realm of global affairs.

As a result, it is not enough to select someone with qualities that fit just national needs when the stakes are planetary, too. The future of the world depends on a strong, just, and fair America.

It is embodied in history, traditions, and institutions and in the presidency. When America has failed to provide strength and integrity, and failed to champion social justice, the entire world failed, as well.

With all its problems and weaknesses, the United States remains an example of democracy, pluralism, and impartiality.

People and nations look to America to provide a model of freedom and fairness. U.S. culture is imitated, examined, and studied around the world. American laws, ideas, and ideals are emulated globally.

As a result, the U.S. is a lighthouse in the darkness for millions who live beyond our shores.

It is a responsibility. We should not shrink from it. We should embrace the task even if we are not without flaws. There is no one else on earth to offer the proper democratic vision and leadership for our globe but the United States of America.

We have no choice. If we fail, the domestic and international forces of intolerance and tyranny will prevail. Our survival is at stake. It is also at risk for those who look to us for leadership across the world.

Since this is the case, we should do all we can to do our part with wisdom, understanding, and strength. We have a duty to provide the best leadership possible to a world that is seeking direction based on the principles represented in the American Bill of Rights.

We are not perfect, but should strive for perfection. Our leaders are not saints, but should seek to be models of integrity. They should be expected to do the right thing, even if it is not the right time. We will never solve all our problems, but we should work to overcome them in good faith and honesty. This will not always be the case, but with proper leadership we can try to resolve the great issues that affect our lives, and the earth we inhabit, with fairness, liberty, justice, and reason. The American presidency symbolizes these principles.

We Elect a Government When We Elect a President

We should realize that we do not elect just a President, but we also elect an entire government. The Chief Executive of America appoints thousands who administer the apparatus of the largest bureaucracy on earth. Those appointees should reflect the same leadership traits of those who appointed them to roles of public trust. The process of voicing the qualities we need should be from "the bottom up" and not "the top down." By this we mean that we, the people, should express ourselves as to what we believe best represents our needs, our ideals, and our model for leadership in the United States and all democracies.

Select and Not Settle for Our Leaders

Courtesy of Pat Oliphant, June 15, 2004, Universal/Uclick[11]

Often, leadership options come from the political establishment. Voters are given predetermined selections. Today, social media improves our choices and gives us control, if we are willing to use it.

We are all connected.

Modern communications provide new platforms for groups and individuals even from the bottom to speak, debate, convey, and vent feelings. We need to vote in a smarter and more intelligent way for the most important positions in our land.

---

[11] The Atlantic, Legendary Cartoonist Pat Oliphant, "We Are in a Forest of Ignorance" (http://www.theatlantic.com/politics/archive/2014/09/legendary-cartoonist-pat-oliphant-we-are-in-a-forest-fire-of-ignorance/379524/)

We should encourage discussion from the classroom to the community to the talk shows and all forms of media, until it is clear that we will select and not settle for anyone but the best and brightest to be President of the United States and the top leaders of our nation.

If one asks, what is the one quality above all that a president must have? By far, the answer should be: Character.

What do we mean by this?

Character includes integrity, honesty, truthfulness, and a moral compass. It predicts behavior.

If we assume a candidate is experienced, communicates well, has presence, charisma, emotional intelligence, and confidence, then the overriding quality to look for is character.

Character and other traits are essential for Americans to trust the nuclear button, their lives, their fortunes, and their sacred honor, and those of the people of the world to the person who will sit at the Resolute Desk in the White House.

We listen to commentators and politicians and their proxies. We talk to friends and family, and then we make our prediction.

Our vote is a forecast about the future.

It is destiny in our hands.

PART ONE: The American Presidency
CHAPTER TWO: ▬▬▬▬▬▬▬▬▬▬▬▬▬▬▬
What to Look For?

> *"The President is merely the most important among a large number of public servants. He should be supported or opposed exactly to the degree which is warranted by his good conduct or bad conduct, his efficiency or inefficiency in rendering loyal, able, and disinterested service to the Nation as a whole. Therefore it is absolutely necessary that there should be full liberty to tell the truth about his acts, and this means that it is exactly necessary to blame him when he does wrong as to praise him when he does right. Any other attitude in an American citizen is both base and servile. To announce that there must be no criticism of the president, or that we are to stand by the president, right or wrong, is not only unpatriotic and servile, but is morally treasonable to the American public. Nothing but the truth should be spoken about him or anyone else. But it is even more important to tell the truth, pleasant or unpleasant, about him than about anyone else."*

— Theodore Roosevelt

In addition to the qualifications we will discuss, there are some general factors we should look for in the candidates:

How they react under stress

How they plan to tackle the big issues

How they conduct themselves on and off the campaign

Personal Presence

We should watch closely *what they have said and what they are saying.*

All of these define them as people and as leaders.

Past and Present words and actions matter.

They catch up with a candidate. They are like torpedoes and dynamite, if not handled properly. They can sink a nominee or explode when least expected. Words exhibit how candidates think and make decisions. They should boost chances for success, or the will contribute to defeat.

Their behavior in and out of the Oval Office matters.

The *San Francisco Chronicle* illustrated some of the most famous campaign gaffes in modern presidential contests in a September 18, 2012, article by Richard Durham entitled: "Top Ten Campaign Gaffes in Modern Presidential History."[12]

The examples include the 2004 race between Senator John Kerry and President George W. Bush. Kerry was attacked for changing his mind on a funding bill. "I actually did vote for the $87 billion, before I voted against it," he explained. The sentence was used by his opponents to define him as a "flip flopper" in the minds of voters and may have contributed to his downfall.

Courtesy of Pat Oliphant, June 15, 2004, Universal/Uclick[11]

---

[12] Richard Durham, "Top Ten Campaign Gaffes in Modern Presidential History," September 18, 2012, San Francisco Chronicle (http://blog.sfgate.com/nov05election/2012/09/18/top-ten-campaign-gaffes-in-mod-ern-presidential-history/)

In the 1972 race to unseat President Richard Nixon, Senator George McGovern had to confront a serious issue. His running mate, vice-presidential nominee Tom Eagleton, had suffered from depression and consequently underwent electric shock therapy. Some top Democrats called for Eagleton to be replaced. McGovern was steadfast in his support: "I am one thousand percent for Tom Eagleton, and I have no intention of dropping him from the ticket," he insisted. Shortly thereafter, McGovern dropped Eagleton as his running mate. His credibility plummeted.

He lost to Nixon in an historic landslide.

In 1976, President Gerald Ford mistakenly stated that Poland was free from the domination of the Soviet Union. It was not. The error haunted Ford throughout the campaign and hurt him with blue collar workers who had families in Eastern Europe. He lost the election to Governor Jimmy Carter of Georgia.

Former Vermont Governor Howard Dean, courtesy Dean for America

During the race for the Democratic nomination for president in 2004, Howard Dean, the one-time front runner, lost the Iowa caucuses.

By Parker, courtesy Florida Today, 2004

In his statement conceding defeat, Dean listed states he had targeted for victory and yelled "Yee-haw." Dean's "Scream" became the key story of the night and helped end his chances for the presidency.

Senator Obama, during the 2008 presidential race, attempted to explain the frustrations of blue collar workers during a fund raiser with wealthy Democrats in San Francisco by saying:

And it's not surprising that they get bitter, they cling to guns or religion or antipathy to people who aren't like them or anti-immigrant sentiment or anti-trade sentiment as a way to explain their frustrations.

As President, Obama was often criticized for the comment.

President Lyndon Johnson and Senator Barry Goldwater, courtesy Library of Congress

The 1964 race between President Lyndon Johnson and Senator Barry Goldwater was a test between conservative and liberal views. Moderate and swing voters were important for both candidates. Goldwater's acceptance speech for his party's nomination became a classic example of how to alienate voters. He said:

Those who do not care for our cause, we don't expect to enter our ranks in any case. And let our Republicanism, so focused and so dedicated, not be made fuzzy and futile by unthinking and stupid labels. I would remind you that extremism in the defense of liberty is no vice. And let me remind you also that moderation in the pursuit of justice is no virtue." [13]

Courtesy Neville Colvin, 1964 Barry Goldwater and Lyndon Johnson Cartoon

---

[13] Barry Goldwater, Republican Convention of 1964 (https://www.youtube.com/watch?v=RVNoCluOh9M)

The Senator from Arizona took six states and 52 electoral votes. The President won with 61% of the popular vote and 486 electoral votes.

Senator Gary Hart, 1987, courtesy of Cornell University

In 1987, rumors began that the Democratic front-runner, Gary Hart, was having affairs. He challenged the media to, "Follow me around." They did. On May 3rd, *The Miami Herald* reported a story about a woman who stayed overnight with Hart.[14] He suspended his campaign a week after and ended his quest for the presidency. A few weeks later, *The National Enquirer* published a photo with him with his alleged girlfriend, Donna Rice, on vacation in Bimini.

---

[14] James Savage, "THE GARY HART STORY: HOW IT HAPPENED," *The Miami Herald* on May 10, 1987 (http://www.unc.edu/~pmeyer/Hart/hartarticle.html)

Governor George Romney, courtesy of
U.S. Department of Housing and Urban Development

Michigan Governor George Romney was an early favorite for the Republican nomination for president in 1968. He was the only anti-Vietnam War Republican candidate among the field that included Ronald Reagan, Nelson Rockefeller, and Richard Nixon. During a TV interview, Romney claimed that his early support of the war was a result of "brainwashing." He said, "When I came back from Vietnam, I just had the greatest brainwashing that anyone can get. Not only by the generals, but also by the diplomatic corps over there. They do a very thorough job." Following the comment, his campaign began to slide.[15]

---

[15] Eric Black | 12/02/11, "Politics by gaffe: Recalling the 'brainwashing' of George Romney," Minneapolis Post, (http://www.minnpost.com/eric-black-ink/2011/12/politics-gaffe-recalling-brainwashing-george-romney)

Vice President Al Gore, courtesy of Library of Congress

"During my service in the United States Congress, I took the initiative in creating the Internet." This statement by Tennessee Democrat Al Gore in a CNN interview on March 9, 1999, cast an image as an exaggerator, which damaged his prospects for the election.[16]

---

[16] Glenn Kessler, November 4, 2013, "A cautionary tale for politicians: Al Gore and the 'invention' of the Internet," *The Washington Post*, (https://www.washingtonpost.com/blogs/fact-checker/wp/2013/11 /04/ a-cautionary-tale-for-politicians-al-gore-and-the-invention-of-the-internet/)

Arkansas Governor Bill Clinton and President George H. W. Bush
during the 1992 campaign, courtesy of Library of Congress

George H.W. Bush won the Republican nomination for president in 1988.
During his acceptance speech, he said, "Read my lips: no new taxes." The
phrase became an important part of his campaign for the presidency,
which he won.

Item: Former President Bush endorses McCain...

Courtesy of Dave Granlund, *Metro West Daily News*

Later, when President Bush agreed to raise taxes to lower the budget deficit, the statement came back to haunt him. He regretted the decision during the 1992 campaign for the Republican nomination when his opponent, Pat Buchanan, used it consistently as an example of Bush's broken promises. That year, President Bush was defeated in his bid for a second term by Arkansas Governor William Jefferson Clinton.

President Richard Nixon, courtesy of *The Atlantic*

To commemorate the 40th anniversary of Richard Nixon's "last press conference," Ethan Rarick of *The San Francisco Chronicle* wrote this on December 1, 2002:[17]

> *On the morning after losing a bid to become governor of California in 1962, Richard Nixon bitterly bid farewell to the political world and the troublesome press corps that chronicled it: "You won't have Nixon to kick around anymore."*
>
> *Usually that "last press conference" is read as a reflection of the man, a hint of the paranoid style that would mark Nixon's presidency.*

Even if elected to office, what he or she has said and done in the past may foretell how they will govern. Their statements could also force their administration to be on the defensive, fighting misstatements and ghosts of the past when they need to concentrate resources on the future.

We need to look cautiously at those candidates who speak without self-control and play fast and loose with facts. It will come back to haunt them and those who voted for them.

Personal Presence

A leader must be engaged with those they lead. This deals with constituents and customers and followers. For example, Lincoln visited his cabinet heads, stayed with the troops, was on the battlefield.

He went to Richmond, immediately after the treaty was signed to end the Civil War, to sit in the chair of Jefferson Davis. He did not cheer or gloat over victory. He was there as a symbol to those who fought, died, and sacrificed. He represented compassion, understanding, and a singular commitment to the ideals that were struggled over.

Eminent leaders are personally present and out front, and they look and exhibit that they are in command.

---

[17] Ethan Rarick, *San Francisco Chronicle*, "Kicking Nixon Around Some More," December 1, 2002 (http://www.sfgate.com/politics/article/Kicking-Nixon-around-some-more-Tricky-Dick-s-2749199.php)

They meet with their teams, discuss issues, and have the discipline to show engagement at all levels. Some may call it casting a perception of leadership. Others say it is cultivating charisma. Others consider it managing power.

To a large extent, it is the rigor to create a self-image that adheres to rules that lead to better handling of the decision-making process. Presidents, Prime Ministers, celebrities and captains of industry and business, look to portray a persona in the eyes of those they command and those who look to them as models. All eyes are on them. Leaders need to be cognizant of 'living in a fishbowl.' All see how they act, speak, and look, all the time. Their lives and personal conduct must reflect the sincerity of their words and actions.

By being personally engaged with their teams, great leaders help develop their subordinates into future leaders. They gain loyalty and respect. Great leaders are accessible and available. When associates stop doing this, then the leader no longer leads."[18]

The Blackmail Factor

We cannot afford to have in the presidency someone with a questionable background who has played loose with morals. Some feel that the sexual escapades of a president are a private affair. They are not. Neither are their financial affairs or other activities that could affect the trust that the public and the world has in them. The president (or any high-level public official, for that matter) can be "blackmailed" and thus controlled by someone or some other country for any real or even perceived weaknesses.

Imagine if political enemies or foreign powers knew of a president's extra marital affairs and used this information to alter vital public policy. It could impact the future of the nation and the world and put in jeopardy countless lives.

It is clear: Words and behavior in and out of the Oval Office do, in fact, matter.

---

[18] Emilio Iodice, *Profiles in Leadership: From Caesar to Modern Times*, North American Business Press: Miami, FL, 2013, p. 282

PART ONE: The American Presidency
CHAPTER THREE: ▬▬▬▬▬▬▬
A Great Country Needs Great Leaders

There is nothing wrong with America that cannot be cured by what is right with America.

— William J. Clinton

What the people want is amazingly simple. They want an America as good as its promise.

— Barbara Jordan

This nation will remain the land of the free only so long as it is the home of the brave.

— Elmer Davis

This country will not be a good place for any of us to live in unless we make it a good place for all of us to live in.

— Theodore Roosevelt

America is a nation with many flaws, but hopes so vast that only the cowardly would refuse to acknowledge them.

— James Michener

When an American says that he loves his country, he means not only that he loves the New England hills, the prairies glistening in the sun, the wide and rising plains, the great mountains, and the sea. He means that he loves an inner air, an inner light in which freedom lives and in which a man can draw the breath of self-respect ... America is much more than a geographical fact. It is a political and moral fact — the first community in which men set out in principle to institutionalize freedom, responsible government, and human equality.

— Adlai Stevenson

If our country is worth dying for in time of war, let us resolve that it is utterly worth living for in time of peace.

— Hamilton Fish

America was born in outrageous ambition, so bold as to be improbable. The deprived, the oppressed, and the powerless from all over the globe came here with little more than the desire to realize themselves.

— Mario Cuomo

Statue of Liberty, courtesy of National Archives

Candidates often claim that they should be selected to the highest office in the land to "make America great again." This assumes that the United States is no longer a country of opportunity and freedom, providing an environment for individual and collective aspirations to be realized. This is not the case if we examine who we are today, where we have been, and where we are going in the context of our American identity.

A July 3, 2014, article in the *Times of San Diego* by Len Novarro,[19] entitled, "America: What Makes It Great," outlined these elements of the American identify:

Technology and Creativity: Some of the greatest inventions of all time have been created by Americans. From Thomas Edison to Steve Jobs, from light bulbs to the Internet, we have constantly developed new ideas for the world. Look at Silicon Valley's billionaires to see how much more is to come from America. Look at how many Americans continue to win Nobel Prizes.

Diversity, Tolerance, Individualism: The Statue of Liberty has written on it: "Give me your tired, your poor, your huddled masses yearning to breathe free . . . ." We have embraced immigrants and people of all faiths and nationalities who want a better life, including our Native Americans, who have inspired us with their desire to work and their generosity. We tolerate each other despite out differences. We are not perfect, but seek perfection. We live together in peace, which is not the case in many parts of the world. Ours is not a class system. Wealth has its influence here, but we still have a society where we can determine our own course.

Economy and Entrepreneurship: We still manage the largest economy on earth, which promotes small business and self-made people. If wealth is a measure, America has more millionaires and billionaires than any other country. And we still have the highest standard of living in the world.

---

[19] Len Novarro, "What Makes America Great," Times of San Diego, July 3, 2014. (http://timesofsandiego.com/opinion/2014/07/03/america-makes-great/)

Our System of Law: Democracy and respect for the law and fairness are part of the American system of government. Our institutions exist to protect both the grand and the humble.

Education: It is not perfect and needs constant improvement, yet our system of education attracts people from the entire globe.

Music and Entertainment: The American contribution to music and movies is enormous, which continues to thrive and grow.

A Nation of Beauty: From coast to coast and from the Great Lakes to the Gulf of Mexico, the U.S. is a country of contrasts and great beauty.

Cities: Some of the most interesting cities on earth are in America. New York, San Francisco, Los Angeles, Chicago, Miami, New Orleans, Boston, and Seattle, for example, are all quite different and full of life and culture.

Sense of Morality and Social Consciousness: We bring out our problems so we can do something about them. We have a sense of doing the right thing despite the obstacles we face to do so.

Remember the Greatest Generation: What made them great? They faced huge problems, first of poverty in the Depression, and then winning the War. They defeated poverty and Nazism. The leaders of that era were not afraid to ask us to sacrifice for a cause they were willing to die for. It was that generation which pulled the country together, and it was those leaders who said, "Follow Me."

Resilience: After almost 250 years of trials, tribulations, and progress, we are still here in much the same form created by the American Revolution.

In the movie, Independence Day, the President said, "We can't be consumed by our petty differences anymore. We will be united in our common interests . . . . We will not go quietly into the night."

And Gary Shapiro, CEO of the Consumer Electronics Association, wrote this in a July 12, 2012, article in Forbes,[20] titled, "Is America the Greatest Country in the World?"

> *I am passionate that our nation was, still is, and can remain the best in world. We not only owe it to our children to act to preserve our greatness, but we must also honor those who have served and risked their life and limb in our Armed Forces to preserve our nation and its freedoms.*
>
> *We are a beacon for the world. Our challenge is not to lament our decline or even celebrate our exceptionalism; it is to come together with true leadership that can unite us as we sacrifice to preserve and expand our greatness.*

Courtesy of Pat Oliphant, Cartoon of September 13, 2001, Universal Uclick

---

[20] Gary Shapiro, "Is America the Greatest Country in the World?", *Forbes*, July 12, 2012 (//www.forbes.com/sites/garyshapiro/2012/07/25/is-america-the-greatest-country-in-the-world/"

We have no other means of self-defense than our solidarity and our knowledge that the cause for which we are suffering is a momentous and sacred cause.

— Albert Einstein

Most of the important things in the world have been accomplished by people who have kept on trying when there seemed to be no hope at all.

— Dale Carnegie

The ultimate measure of a man (and a woman) is not where he (or she) stands in moments of comfort and convenience, but where he stands at times of challenge and controversy.

— Martin Luther King, Jr.

*Promise me you'll always remember: You're braver than you believe, and stronger than you seem, and smarter than you think. (*Christopher Robin to Pooh*)*

— A.A.Milne

When the going gets tough, the tough get going.

— Francis Leahy

PART TWO: Leadership Qualities of The Commander in Chief
CHAPTER ONE: ▰▰▰▰▰▰▰▰▰▰▰▰
Reformer

There is a need for financial reform along ethical lines that would produce in its turn an economic reform to benefit everyone. This would nevertheless require a courageous change of attitude on the part of political leaders.

— Pope Francis

To live for a principle, for the triumph of some reform by which all mankind are to be lifted up to be wedded to an idea may be, after all, the holiest and happiest of marriages.

— Elizabeth Cady Stanton

Whenver anything extraordinary is done in American municipal politics, whether for good or for evil, you can trace it almost invariably to one man. The people do not do it. Neither do the 'gangs,' 'combines,' or political parties.

—Lincoln Steffens

Let my name stand among those who are willing to bear ridicule and reproach for the truth's sake, and so earn some right to rejoice when the victory is won.

— Louisa May Alcott

Men must be capable of imagining and executing and insisting on social change if they are to reform or even maintain civilization, and capable too of furnishing the rebellion which is sometimes necessary if society is not to perish of immobility.

—Rebecca West

Bram Stoker wrote in his diary: '[Theodore Roosevelt] must be president someday. A man you cannot cajole, cannot frighten, can't buy.'

— Edmund Morris, *The Rise of Theodore Roosevelt*

Nobody cares how much you know until they know how much you care.

— Theodore Roosevelt

President Theodore Roosevelt, courtesy of Library of Congress

One of the words most frequently used in presidential politics is "reform." Candidates invariably claim that they will be the ones to reform the system. In nearly every election cycle in the last 30 years, candidates have focused on health care reform, tax reform, immigration reform, campaign financing reform, entitlement reform, etc. Some progress has been made in these areas, but more, arguably, needs to be done. What is obvious is that one trait that is essential to be an effective American president is to be a true and experienced reformer. Take the perennial issue of campaign finance reform as an example.

Theodore Roosevelt fought to reform the method of financing and conducting political campaigns as far back as 1881 as a New York state assemblyman.

Theodore Roosevelt: Civil Service, Campaign and Economic Reform

In the Mission Statement of the U.S. Office of Personnel Management, there is the biography of Theodore Roosevelt. He is considered the greatest Civil Service Commissioner in American history. As Commissioner, Roosevelt accomplished major revisions to the way the Federal Government functioned and hired public servants, especially the operation of the "spoils system:"[21]

> *With unbridled courage, zeal, and tenacity, Theodore Roosevelt worked to ensure a hiring system for America's government workers based on fairness and equal access and protection for all—making him the undisputed father of today's Federal Service. During his term as United States Civil Service Commissioner (1889-1895), the full force of his energy, enthusiasm, and aggressiveness was put to the task of building up the Federal civil service system.*
>
> *He undertook the task of reform with the same honesty and zeal that he showed for all his endeavors. Commissioner Roosevelt believed his role was to create a civil service system that would attract the best people into government.*

Roosevelt's principles to reform the system were based on three standards: (1) nondiscrimination and opportunities for all citizens, (2) merit-based appointments, and (3) shielding public servants from punishment because of their political beliefs. He led the fight to expose corrupt officials and toiled against waste, fraud, and abuse.

On one occasion, he personally recommended the removal of New York board examiners who sold test questions to the public for $50.

He had Baltimore postal officials arrested for buying votes for the re-election of the man who had appointed him to his position, President Benjamin Harrison.

---

[21] U.S. Office of Personnel Management, "Mission Statement 2015" (https://www.opm.gov/about-us/our-mission-role-history/theodore-roosevelt/)

His courage and tenacity assured that civil service laws would be permanently enforced, no matter what political affiliation.[22]

"Conservative radicals, like Hamilton, Lincoln, and T.R., begin with moderate dispositions. They have a reverence for the collective wisdom of the past. They have an awareness that the veneer of civilization is thin and if you simply start breaking things you get nihilism, not progress. They are acutely aware of the complexity of the world, and how limited our knowledge of it is. They are pragmatists, experimenters, liberals. But they also understand that in moments of historical transition, it is prudent to be bold. They understand that when your society is crumbling, the only way to restore stability is to address the problems that are breaking it."[23]

Courtesy of National Archives

As President, Theodore Roosevelt led one of the greatest expansions and modernizations of the government. The competitive civil service grew from 110,000 to 235,000. As a result, the merit system far surpassed the spoils system in numbers in federal hiring.

For the first time, African Americans and minorities entered the government, allowing thousands of families to rise above poverty while providing important services to the nation.

---

[22] Ibid. Office of Personnel Management
[23] David Brooks, "This Is Where I Stand," *The New York Times*, August 15, 2020 (https://www.nytimes.com/section/opinion)

Woodrow Wilson, who became president in 1913, changed this. Through the power of the presidency, he reversed the opportunities given to minorities via the Civil Service and relegated them to second class citizenship.

NO MOLLY-CODDLING HERE

Courtesy of National Archives

Theodore Roosevelt fought to control monopolistic power in business, created the Departments of Commerce and Labor, and added 150 million acres of public lands to be conserved as part of the nation's national parks. And he proposed and signed new laws to regulate the pharmaceutical industry, as well as rules to protect the health of the people of America. Roosevelt's 1906 Pure Food and Drug Act remains the foundation of the U.S. system of health into the 21st century.

The Office of President Theodore Roosevelt, 1904, courtesy of Library of Congress

Roosevelt built the West Wing of the White House to be the executive office of the president, which today houses the Oval Office. His changes ushered in the modern American Presidency. An issue that is still being discussed is altering the way we finance campaigns. Beth Rowen, in an essay in the *Infoplease Almanac*, titled "*Campaign-Finance Reform: History and Timeline*"[24], wrote the following:

> *Over the past several decades, political campaigns in the U.S. have become increasingly costly and unsavory. Nevertheless, campaign finance remains a divisive issue. Proponents of campaign finance limits argue that wealthy donors and corporations hold too much sway in elections and, as a result, corrupt campaigns. Those favoring less regulation contend that campaign donations are a form of free speech.*

> *Campaign finance legislation dates to 1867, but the regulation of campaign fundraising didn't become a major issue until the early 20th Century, prompted by the presidential election of 1896, which introduced a new era of campaign advertising and the custom of seeking donations from businesses.*

---

[24] Beth Rowen, *Infoplease Almanac 2015*, "Campaign Finance Reform: History and Timeline" (http://www. infoplease.com/us/history/campaign-finance-reform-timeline.html)

*The Whiff of Corruption in Campaigns Not a New Phenomenon
Patronage was prevalent in early campaigns, and the spoils system
was in full swing by the time Andrew Jackson took office in 1828.
Jackson was famous for appointing contributors to plum positions in
his administration. The spoils system factored into the assassination
of James Garfield. One of the president's supporters and speech
writers, Charles Guiteau, shot and killed Garfield after being denied a
post in his administration.*

*The assassination led to passage of the Pendleton Act of 1883,
which required that civil service positions be filled based on merit
and exam results rather than party affiliation.*

*Vote-buying was another form of corruption in early presidential
races. Political parties and candidates printed their own ballots and
often paid voters to submit them. The government did not take
responsibility for printing ballots until 1896.*

*The movement to rein in campaign fundraising and spending gathered
steam once again after Watergate, when corruption in politics reached
its peak and public confidence in public officials hit a nadir.*

There have been presidents who have been successful in changing the
system to righting wrongs and correcting abuses to the political process.
This is one quality that is needed, especially with challenges that seem
impossible to overcome, like campaign financing, immigration reform, and
tax reform. It has been attempted in the past, not always successfully.

Beth Rowen, in the article previously cited, outlined some of the
legislation of the past that worked to reform the system of financing
political campaigns.

During the administration of Theodore Roosevelt (1900-1908), for
example, the Tillman Act was passed to prohibit corporations and
national banks from financing presidential and congressional campaigns.
It was the first law to regulate federal campaigns, but it was filled with
loopholes that made it less effective than originally planned.

The first federal campaign disclosure law was passed in 1910 during the term of William Howard Taft (1908-1912). The Federal Corrupt Practices Act required candidates for the House of Representatives to disclose the source of all contributions and report on campaign spending. It was later amended to also require Senators to adhere to the same guidelines.

Restrictions were tightened, with legislation leading almost to the present day. In recent years, major reversals from Supreme Court decisions have once again resulted in demands for reform.

Byron Tau, in an article in *The Wall Street Journal*, titled, "Campaign Finance Reform, An Enduring Election Promise", explained the following: [25]

After the 2002 Bipartisan Campaign Reform Act, some campaign cash started flowing to outside groups that were required under law to remain independent of parties and candidates. In exchange for that independence, they could spend freely. In 2004 and 2008, these groups were called 527s. [italicize and indent, like following parags since quote]

In subsequent years, federal courts have affirmed and expanded the right of outside groups to spend in politics, and super PAC and the 501(c) 4 nonprofits became their favored vehicles.

Since then, critics of the system have proposed a constitutional amendment to give Congress the power to regulate and stem the flow of money into politics.

"The flood of dark money into our nation's political system poses the greatest threat to our democracy that I have witnessed during my time in public service," Sen. Harry Reid (D Nevada) said at a hearing last year.

Reid's statement is telling. The lifeblood of democracy is citizen participation, with government held accountable to the people. Our current system of campaign financing depends on big contributors. It has weakened public participation and accountability.

---

[25] Byron Tau, "Campaign Finance Reform, An Enduring Election Promise," April 22, 2015, *Wall Street Journal* (http://blogs.wsj.com/washwire/2015/04/22/campaign-finance-reform-an-enduring-election-promise/)

Low voter turnouts, even in high profile elections, cynicism, and lack of trust in politicians and the political process is rampant in the face of influence from wealthy contributors and scandals involving campaign contributions.

The Commander in Chief of the United States must change the system if democracy is to survive and evolve in America.

Abraham Lincoln, 1860, courtesy of Library of Congress

Abraham Lincoln and the Emancipation Proclamation

"'A house divided against itself cannot stand.' I believe this government cannot endure permanently half slave and half free. I do not expect the Union to be dissolved – I do not expect the house to fall – but I do expect it will cease to be divided. It will become all one thing, or all the other.

"As I would not be a slave, so I would not be a master. This expresses my idea of democracy. Whatever differs from this, to the extent of the difference, is no democracy.

"It is the eternal struggle between two principles – right and wrong – throughout the world. They are the two principles that have stood face to face from the beginning of time; and will ever continue to struggle. The one is the common right of humanity, and the other the divine right of kins. It is the same principle in whatever shape it develops itself.

"Let us have faith that right makes might, and in that faith, let us, to the end, dare to do our duty as we understand it.

"In giving freedom to the slave, we assure freedom to the free — honorable alike in what we give, and what we preserve. We shall nobly save, or meanly lose, the last best hope of earth. Other means may succeed; this could not fail. The way is plain, peaceful, generous, just — a way which, if followed, the world will forever applaud, and God must forever bless."

I have always thought that all men should be free; but if any should be slaves, it should be first those who desire it for themselves, and secondly those who desire it for others.

— Abraham Lincoln

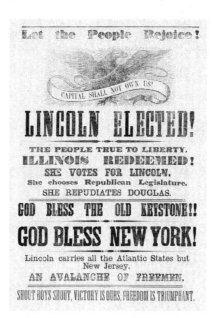

Courtesy of *Harper's Weekly*, November 17, 1860

Dr. Ronald C. White is the foremost biographer of Abraham Lincoln today. His marvelous work, *A. Lincoln: A Biography* (Random House: New York, 2009) was reviewed by Ariel Gonzalez of the *Miami Herald.* He described our sixteenth president this way:

"Abraham Lincoln was less qualified to assume the presidency than any of his 15 predecessors. A self-educated lawyer with only two years in Congress under his belt, he had no executive, diplomatic, or military experience (aside from a few uneventful months in the Illinois state militia). Even so, he successfully led the nation through its worst crisis .... Lincoln's moral and intellectual development equipped him with the tools he needed for greatness." It was those skills that gave him the wisdom and courage to fight to preserve the individual and collective liberty contained in the U. S. Constitution and our Declaration of Independence.

When Abraham Lincoln joined the newly formed Republican Party, he embraced its principles of reform. They stressed the personal growth of the individual to enjoy freedom and economic opportunity, no matter what one's class or station in life. It was believed that anyone could rise to attain the American dream and that government should work to promote it.

"We stand at once the wonder and admiration of the whole world," he said in 1856. He saw the Republican mission as, "This cause is that every man can make himself." Abraham Lincoln viewed liberty as the economic and social freedom to unleash the genius of the republic to allow all to remake themselves as they desired. He was the embodiment of this reform movement: "There is no permanent class of hired laborers amongst us," Lincoln insisted in 1859:

> *Twenty-five years ago, I was a hired laborer. The hired laborer of yesterday, labors on his own account today; and will hire others to labor for him to-morrow. Advancement — improvement in condition — is the order of things in a society of equals.* [26]

This opportunity had to be extended to all people who inhabited the American continent, including slaves.

---

[26] Lincoln, "Speech at Kalamazoo, Michigan" (August 27, 1856) and "Fragment on Free Labor" (September 17, 1859), in Collected Works, 2:364 and 3:462 (https://www.gilderlehrman.org/history-by-era/lincoln/essays/lincoln)

Writing the Emancipation Proclamation Engraving, Baltimore, October 1862, Adalbert John Volck, artist, courtesy of The Gilder Lehrman Collection, New York

The greatest act of political, social, and economic reform of the 19th century was the abolition of slavery in America. The Emancipation Proclamation bore the name of Abraham Lincoln.

Lincoln was not an abolitionist, yet he believed in eliminating slavery.

It was Lincoln who worked vigorously, intensely, and ruthlessly with a reluctant Congress to pass the 13th Amendment to the Constitution, which ended slavery. It was the major issue dividing the nation and led to the Civil War.

His courage and tenacity as a reformer resulted in the end of human bondage in America.

Top leaders must be courageous reformers who will tackle the great issues of their time that need to change in every democracy.

The range of issues is vast.

It goes from campaign financing, to immigration, to tax policy, to a host of social issues that continue to be in the forefront of public and political concern.

We require Presidents and Prime Ministers who unite us to change what must be changed to make our nations stronger, fairer, and freer.

> *Always bear in mind that your own resolution to succeed is more important than any other one thing.*

— Abraham Lincoln

PART TWO: Leadership Qualities of The Commander in Chief
CHAPTER TWO:
Experience

Experience is the teacher of all things.

— Julius Caesar

People grow through experience if they meet life honestly and courageously. This is how character is built.

— Eleanor Roosevelt

One thorn of experience is worth a whole wilderness of warning.

— James Russell Lowell

The only source of knowledge is experience.

— Albert Einstein

Washington, Jefferson, and Lincoln, courtesy of Miller Center, University of Virginia

The Presidency Is Not a Position for Trainees

The White House is not a place for 'trainees.' Decisions need to be made, at times, in the blink of an eye. The president must be able to judge and decide quickly. There are no comparable jobs to that of president. There are roles that provide preparation.

Theodore Roosevelt and Franklin Roosevelt,
Governors of New York, courtesy of Miller Center, University of Virginia

The Governors

Seventeen U.S. Presidents have been state governors.

Some have been exceptional and, arguably, among our most effective leaders.

They include Thomas Jefferson (Virginia), James Monroe (Virginia), Grover Cleveland (New York), William McKinley (Ohio), Theodore Roosevelt (New York), Woodrow Wilson (New Jersey), Franklin Roosevelt (New York), Ronald Reagan (California), Bill Clinton (Arkansas) and George W. Bush (Texas).

Of course, experience as governor of a large state is different from that of a smaller state. The more complex the region, the more comparable it will be to the setting in the White House. Bringing this form of experience, plus other useful qualities, improves the chances of a successful presidency, but does not ensure it.

Neither Washington nor Lincoln was a state governor. They were exceptions.

Washington brought respect, dignity, military, and administrative skills and admiration as a founding father of our republic. He was present from the Revolution through to the Constitution. He understood the substance of the United States and articulated a clear vision for our future.

Abraham Lincoln brought the wisdom of the prairie and the American heartland. He had little formal education, but he loved learning and understood the human condition.

What Lincoln lacked, he more than made up for with his qualities of compassion, vision, his willingness to make tough decisions, and his spirit of self-sacrifice and dedication to the ideals of American democracy. Abraham Lincoln brought integrity, wisdom, and leadership to the White House as no one before or after him has done.

What is clear is that just experience, per se, is not enough to ensure a successful president. The type, the length, breath, depth, and relevancy of the experience is key, as well as other accompanying qualities like bravery, good judgment, and the ability to communicate and articulate a vision.

One good example is James Buchanan. He was one of the most experienced men to occupy the White House.

James Buchanan, President of the United States, 1856-1860, courtesy Library of Congress

James Buchanan: Considered One of Our Worst Leaders

Buchanan was elected five times to the House of Representatives. He spent ten years in the Senate. He was the Minister to Russia under President Andrew Jackson, the Minister to Great Britain during the administration of President Franklin Pierce, and the Secretary of State under President James K. Polk.

His time abroad and in the capitol helped him secure the Democratic nomination for President in 1856. He was certainly a candidate who was knowledgeable and understood the role of President. He aspired to be compared to George Washington. Instead, Buchanan ranks among our worst Chief Executives in the eyes of many historians.[27]

Buchanan spent most of his time outside the U.S. when the great debates about sectional politics and slavery occurred. So he did not understand the underlying issues. He used diplomacy to maintain peace between the North and South, which resulted in alienating both sides. He viewed secession as illegal, but felt that going to war was also illegal. As a result, he failed to create a unifying principle that the Northern and Southern states could both accept to preserve the Union.[28]

President Polk considered Buchanan a man who lacked judgment. His political enemies said most of his ventures did not materialize, like the expansion of the Navy and the Army. They claimed that he missed the key opportunities of his age by vetoing the Morrill Act and the Homestead Act. The first accelerated agriculture and engineering research and education, and the latter opened the west.

Both were signed into law by Abraham Lincoln a few years later.[29]

---

[27] Philip S. Klein, *President James Buchanan: A Biography,* American Political Biography Press: Newtown, Connecticut, 1995, p. 305
[28] Ibid. Klein p. xviii
[29] Ibid. Klein, p. 62

The Value of Business Experience

Several presidents had business experience before entering the White House, which might have been of benefit to the position in the Oval Office.

What we find is that it does not always translate into the kind of skill that fits well in the White House. Much more depends on other factors than just business experience per se.

President Abraham Lincoln with youngest son,
Tad, courtesy of the Library of Congress

Abraham Lincoln

Lincoln ran a general store and invented a device to raise riverboats over sandbars, making him the only president to receive a patent. He also operated a successful law practice. He was characterized by determination and resilience, even in the face of chronic failure.

Courtesy of the Library of Congress

Warren G. Harding

At 19, Harding bought a small newspaper business in Ohio, *The Marion Star*. He managed the operation with his wife, and it became a financial success.

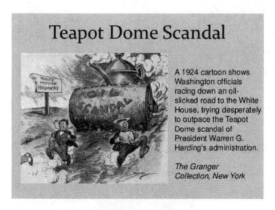

Courtesy of the Granger Collection, New York, and the National Archives

Harding, according to presidential historians, ranks along with James Buchanan as among our least successful presidents.

President Herbert Hoover with his dog, King Tut, courtesy of Library of Congress

Herbert Hoover

After graduating from Stanford University with a degree in geology, Herbert Hoover started his own mining and engineering business in 1908. His company employed 175,000 people. It reorganized failing firms and invested in new projects.

Political Cartoon depicting Herbert Hoover's challenges, courtesy of National Archives

Hoover was elected to the White House in 1928. The Wall Street Crash happened a year later.

He was unable to deal with the Great Depression that ensued. Millions lost their jobs and thousands of firms and institutions literally disappeared, creating the worst economic and social crisis in U.S. history.

He was swept out of office by Franklin Roosevelt in the election of 1932.

Courtesy of Library of Congress

Franklin Delano Roosevelt

Franklin Roosevelt was still a young man when he was struck with infantile paralysis. He went to a resort in Warm Springs, Georgia, to find relief. After a short time, he decided to invest part of his inherited trust fund into an operation to help others rise from polio.

Poster featuring FDR to raise funds for Polio research,
courtesy of Franklin Delano Roosevelt Presidential Library

He created the Roosevelt Warm Springs Institute for Rehabilitation in
1927. It is still operating today, a medical center serving thousands of
patients each year.

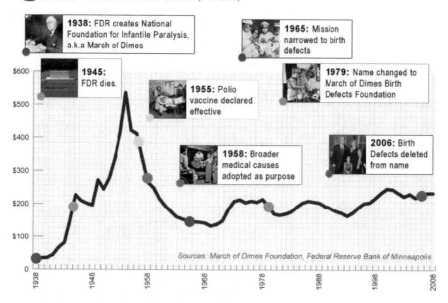

The March *of* Numbers
Annual donations in 2008 dollars (millions)

1938: FDR creates National Foundation for Infantile Paralysis, a.k.a March of Dimes

1945: FDR dies.

1955: Polio vaccine declared effective

1958: Broader medical causes adopted as purpose

1965: Mission narrowed to birth defects

1979: Name changed to March of Dimes Birth Defects Foundation

2006: Birth Defects deleted from name

Sources: March of Dimes Foundation, Federal Reserve Bank of Minneapolis

March of Dimes Today, courtesy of *Forbes* Magazine

Courtesy of the White House

Harry Truman

When Harry Truman returned from France at the end of World War I, he needed a job. He opened a clothing store with a wartime buddy. It flourished for several years, but ended when a recession forced it to close.

Courtesy of George H.W. Presidential Library

George H.W. Bush

Following his time at Yale, the future 41st president formed Bush-Overby Oil Development Company in 1951. In a few years, the firm merged with Zapata Petroleum, resulting in a remarkably successful venture.

Courtesy of George W. Bush Presidential Library

George W. Bush

President George W. Bush owned the Texas Rangers baseball team. He was phenomenally successful in increasing the value of his investment, which made him a wealthy man.

Courtesy of the Jimmy Carter Presidential Library

Jimmy Carter

Jimmy Carter inherited a failing peanut farm when his father died in 1953. Carter resigned from the Navy to return to Georgia and take over the family business. He worked hard and diligently, and he applied strong management skills to produce a business that became prosperous.

Wendell Willkie: First Major Business Leader to Run for President

Wendell L. Willkie 1940, courtesy of Indiana Historical Society

"I am in business and proud of it...Nobody can make me soft-pedal any fact in my business career. After all, business is our way of life, our achievement, our glory.

"The only soil in which liberty can grow is that of a united people. We must have faith that the welfare of one is the welfare of all. We must know that the truth can only be reached by the expression of our free opinions, without fear and without rancor. We must acknowledge that all are equal before God and before the law. And we must learn to abhor those disruptive pressures, whether religious, political, or economic, that the enemies of liberty employ.

> *When Winston Churchill became Prime Minister of England a few months ago, he made no sugar-coated promises. 'I have nothing to offer you,' he said, 'but blood, tears, toil, and sweat.' Those are harsh words, brave words; yet if England lives, it will be because her people were told the truth and accepted it. Fortunately, in America, we are not reduced to 'blood and tears.' But we shall not be able to avoid the 'toil and sweat.'*

— Wendell Willkie

He was the Republican Party Nominee for President in 1940. Willkie was a business leader and proud of it. It was the first time in American history that someone of Willkie's background won the nomination for president from a major political party. He was a successful lawyer, World War I veteran, and head of one of the largest electric utility companies in the country, Commonwealth and Southern. He was a former Democrat, but changed his party affiliation during the New Deal. He actively opposed FDR's economic policies.

Without having any professional political experience, Willkie vigorously sought the nomination of the Republican Party for President in 1940. Not all Republicans were delighted to learn this. That Willkie was a former Democrat and was seeking the nomination of the opposing party's highest office ran against the grain of the Republican Party's rank and file.

A senator from his home state of Indiana, James Watson, said he didn't mind if the town whore joined the church, but she should not lead the choir the first week.[30]

---

[30] James H. Madison (February 2001), "Willkie, Wendell Lewis" *American National Biography*, retrieved November 5, 2015

The daughter of the late Republican President Theodore Roosevelt, Alice Roosevelt Longworth, said the Willkie campaign was "from the grass roots of ten thousand country clubs."[31]

Willkie won the nomination on the sixth ballot at a highly charged Republican convention, defeating several veteran politicians, including Senators Robert A. Taft of Ohio and Arthur Vandenberg of Michigan, as well as the young New York District Attorney, Thomas E. Dewey. The great issue during the convention was the war in Europe, which began in 1939.

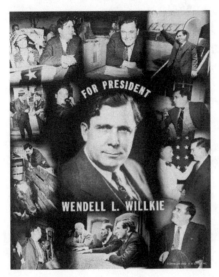

Wendell Willkie Campaign Poster, 1940, courtesy of Library of Congress

Willkie campaigned on the theme that he would be better able to handle a national emergency and would also bring the nation back to prosperity. He emphasized that his business and executive leadership prepared him well to take on the economic and foreign policy challenges facing the nation. He styled himself after a common mid-westerner seeking the support of working class voters.

---

[31] Steve Neal, *Dark Horse: A Biography of Wendell Willkie,* Doubleday: Garden City, NY, 1984, p. 40

FDR's Interior Secretary, Harold L. Ickes, poked fun at Willkie by calling him "a simple, barefoot Wall Street lawyer."[32] Roosevelt had considered the idea of retiring, but saw the war looming large in the destiny of the United States. He decided to seek an unprecedented third term. In the end, FDR was re-elected. Willkie received 45% of the popular vote, but carried only nine states. When the outcome was clear, FDR confided to his son James: "I'm happy I've won, but I'm sorry Wendell lost."[33]

After the election, Willkie decided he would do all he could to support the president's efforts to aid Britain. He announced his support of the Lend-Lease Program on January 13th, 1941, only two months after conceding defeat to FDR. The President appreciated Willkie's talents and willingness to serve the country. FDR felt it was necessary to show bi-partisan support for the United Kingdom by sending the nominal head of the opposition party as his emissary to support the British war effort. The Republicans were highly opposed to Lend-Lease. Willkie's announcement created a firestorm of protest against him from the party regulars.

Nevertheless, he visited the President on the eve of FDR's third swearing in to discuss his new role. The President appointed him as his emissary to Britain and gave him a confidential letter to personally deliver to Winston Churchill. Willkie left for London three days later. His trip received great notoriety on both sides of the Atlantic. Willkie promised to do all he could to help Britain in her struggle against Nazi Germany. He saw the damage caused by the Blitzkrieg bombings of London, Coventry, Birmingham, and Liverpool.

He walked through the streets of London during Nazi raids and visited shelters. Churchill met with Willkie and recalled "a long talk with this most able and forceful man."[34] Willkie returned to the U.S., and his mission was deemed a triumph.

Willkie gave FDR full support for his efforts before and after Pearl Harbor. FDR decided to run for a fourth term. He wanted to remove Vice President Henry Wallace from the ticket. He sent an intermediary to ask Willkie if he would be interested in taking on the role. Willkie never responded. Instead,

[32] Richard Moe, *Roosevelt's Second Act* Oxford: Oxford University Press, 2013
[33] Ibid. p.179-180

he made an attempt to secure the Republican nomination for president in 1944, but bowed out after a disappointing showing in the Wisconsin primary. Governor Thomas E. Dewey was the Republican nominee, and Roosevelt once again won re-election.

Willkie and FDR talked about forming a new liberal party after the war. His vision and dreams were snuffed out when he suddenly died in October 1944, at the age of 52. His legacy was his staunch support of Roosevelt's plan to support Britain and his courage in the face of strong political opposition.

Susan Dunn wrote of Willkie: "He died as he had lived, an idealist, a humanitarian, and a lone wolf."[35] Steve Neal, Willkie's biographer, explained something even more profound about him:

"Though he never became President, he had won something much more important: a lasting place in American history. Along with Henry Clay, William Jennings Bryan, and Hubert Humphrey, he was the also-ran who would be long remembered.

"'He was a born leader,' wrote historian Allan Nevins, 'and he stepped up to leadership at just the moment when the world needed him.' Shortly before his death, Willkie told a friend, 'If I could write my own epitaph and if I had to choose between saying, 'Here lies an unimportant President,' or, 'Here lies one who contributed to saving freedom at a moment of great peril,' I would prefer the latter.'"[36]

The Concept of "Unfiltered Leaders"

Harvard University Professor Gautam Mukunda argues that experience in one role does not automatically transfer to a job like that of President of the United States.

In an article in *Fortune Magazine*, he wrote that Republican Party candidate Mitt Romney's business experience did not necessarily make

---

[34] Ibid. Neal, pp. 195-196
[35] Susan Dunn, *1940: FDR, Willkie, Lindbergh, Hitler—the Election Amid the Storm*. Yale University Press: New Haven, CT, 2013, p. 317

him qualified to take on a political role:[37]

We have a lot of research that tells us experience does not transfer from one context to another very well. We know that when you bring stars from one company to another, even in the same industry, they usually do not stay stars. That is true even when you are moving within an industry. So, think about how much truer it is going to be when you are moving from finance to politics . . . .

The job of someone in a private equity fund is to maximize return on investors' capital. He is incredibly good at that. But the job of president is not to maximize return on investors' capital. The President of the United States has 300 million people he must benefit, and they have lots of different interests.

Can he form coalitions with people who have no reason to work with him? Can he rally the public? Can he negotiate, keeping in mind that he serves many, many different constituencies?

Are you saying that Romney's business experience would be a handicap, not an advantage?

It is both. The business experience tells us he is incredibly smart, he is hardworking, he is analytical. He can solve problems creatively and intelligently. These are all good things in a president. They should give us some confidence that we are not picking someone at random who has never done anything that would make you feel they are capable of being president. But at the same time, it is a profoundly different set of skills.

Professor Mukunda claims that those with business experience alone are prone to mistakes that politicians would not make.

---

[36] Ibid. Neal, p. 324
[37] *Fortune Magazine*, August 24, 2012, "Do Presidents Need Experience," by Gautam Mukunda. (http://fortune.com/2012/08/24/do-presidents-need-experience/)

He believes that "unfiltered leaders"—those who have not much relevant experience—will likely have a greater impact than filtered leaders. "What's harder to predict is whether that impact will be good or bad."[38]

That impact can go either way.

The First Lincoln-Douglas Debate, August 21, 1858, courtesy of The Robinson Library and the National Archives, and Lincoln Home National Historic Site

Abraham Lincoln spent less time in politics than his competitor for the presidency in 1860, Stephen A. Douglas. In Mukunda's analysis, that would make Lincoln "massively unfiltered."

This explains his success. Lincoln had little experience, but produced extraordinary results.

---

[38] Ibid. Mukunda

PART TWO: Leadership Qualities of The Commander in Chief
CHAPTER THREE: ▬▬▬▬▬▬▬
Communicator

Words are singularly the most powerful force available to humanity. We can choose to use this force constructively, with words of encouragement, or destructively, using words of despair. Words have energy and power with the ability to help, to heal, to hinder, to hurt, to harm, to humiliate and to humble.

— Yehuda Berg

Whatever words we utter should be chosen with care, for people will hear them and be influenced by them, for good or ill.

— Buddha

Speak clearly, if you speak at all; carve every word before you let it fall.

— Oliver Wendell Holmes, Sr.

The constant free flow of communication...enabling the free interchange of ideas, forms the very bloodstream of our nation. It keeps the mind and body of our democracy eternally vital, eternally young.

— Franklin D. Roosevelt

I won a nickname, 'The Great Communicator.' But I never thought it was my style or the words I used that made a difference: It was the content. I wasn't a great communicator, but I communicated great things, and they didn't spring full bloom from my brow, they came from the heart of a great nation — from our experience, our wisdom, and our belief in principles that have guided us for two centuries.

— Ronald Reagan

You can fool all the people some of the time, and some of the people all the time, but you cannot fool all the people all the time.

— Abraham Lincoln

At the heart of presidential leadership is the ability to communicate. It can take many forms. In the modern era, "tweeting" and other forms of social media and television have become the "bully pulpit" for chief executives of America and across the world to transmit their messages, their vision for the future, and to sway political and public opinion. Several have done it supremely well and communicated thoughts and ideals that are still with us today.

Abraham Lincoln delivering the Gettysburg Address,
November 19, 1863, courtesy of the Library of Congress

"Fourscore and seven years ago our fathers brought forth on this continent, a new nation, conceived in Liberty, and dedicated to the proposition that all men are created equal...

That this nation, under God, shall have a new birth of freedom – and that government of the people, by the people, for the people, shall not perish from the Earth.

— Lincoln's Gettysburg Address

With malice toward none, with charity for all, with firmness in the right as God gives us to see the right, let us strive on to finish the work we are in, to bind up the nation's wounds, to care for him who shall have borne the battle and for his widow and his orphan, to do all which may achieve and cherish a just and lasting peace among ourselves and with all nations.

— Lincoln's Second Inaugural Address

Abraham Lincoln: The Gettysburg Address and the Second Inaugural Address

Lincoln wrote and delivered a short, yet powerful, speech.

The Gettysburg Address is 2 minutes long.

It is an amazing example of verbal compression. His words, phrases, and sentences are succinct, with few adjectives and no flowery expressions. Historians still study the 270-word talk to find subtle ideas and concepts that continue to be meaningful over 150 years after it was delivered.

Such is also the case with Lincoln's last speech, his Second Inaugural Address.

Ronald C. White's remarkable book, *Lincoln's Greatest Speech: The Second Inaugural* (Simon & Schuster: New York, 2002), describes the setting as Abraham Lincoln spoke:

After four years of unspeakable horror and sacrifice on both sides, the Civil War was about to end. On March 4th, 1865, at his second inauguration, President Lincoln did not offer the North the victory speech it yearned for, nor did he blame the South solely for the sin of slavery. Calling the whole nation to account, Lincoln offered a moral framework for peace and reconciliation. The speech was greeted with indifference, misunderstanding, and hostility by many in the Union. But it was a great work, the victorious culmination of Lincoln's own lifelong struggle with the issue of slavery, and he well understood it to be his most profound speech. Eventually this 'with malice toward none' address would be accepted and revered as one of the greatest in the nation's history . . . . These words, delivered only weeks before his assassination, were the culmination of Lincoln's moral and rhetorical genius.

White described it as Lincoln's "Sermon on the Mount." He said, "In the Sermon on the Mount, Jesus offered a new ethic rooted in humility and compassion: 'blessed are those' who do not follow the way of the

Lincoln delivering his Second Inaugural Address, courtesy of the National Archives

world — judgment — but follows the new way of grace and mercy. In the Second Inaugural, Lincoln offered a surprising ethic of judgment and reconciliation." The speech was the second shortest inaugural address in U.S. history. It was 701 words. He spoke for only six or seven minutes. It was more like a homily than a discourse. In his words he articulated the parameters of winning the peace through reconciliation.

The true test of whether the Civil War was fought for a just cause would be the way we treated those who had been vanquished.

Hatred had to end.

If not, then the savagery and sacrifice would have been to no avail. "The words were practical as well as beautiful. In this final paragraph, Lincoln offered the ultimate surprise. Instead of rallying his supporters, in the name of God, to support the war, he asked his listeners, quietly, to imitate the ways of God."[39]

> *Forty-one days after he delivered the greatest inaugural address in American history, Abraham Lincoln was dead.*
>
> *My favorite thought about Abraham Lincoln is he believed in two things: loving one another and working together to make this world better.*

— Mario Cuomo

---

[39] Ronald C. White, Jr., *Lincoln's Greatest Speech: The Second Inaugural*, Introduction, Simon & Schuster, 2002, as reviewed by David Herbert Donald

"The Great Communicator," courtesy of Reagan Presidential Library

"We cannot help everyone, but everyone can help someone.

"Freedom is never more than one generation away from extinction. We did not pass it to our children in the bloodstream. It must be fought for, protected, and handed on for them to do the same.

> *There are no constraints on the human mind, no walls around the human spirit, and no barriers to our progress except those we ourselves erect.*

— **Ronald Reagan**

Ronald Reagan: The Great Communicator

He was called "The Great Communicator." *The New York Daily News* described him this way:[40]

---

[40] Fred Thompson, *The New York Daily News*, February 11, 2011, "What Made Ronald Reagan the Great Communicator: Former U.S. Senator Fred Thompson Reflects" (http://www.nydailynews.com/opinion/made-ronald-reagan-great-communicator-u-s-senator-fred-thompson-reflects-article-1.133489#ixzz2sZQcziVW)

More than most presidents, Reagan's success was tied directly to his ability not just to speak to the American people, but to communicate with them...but his reputation as The Great Communicator boils down to three basic traits: he was simple; he was clear; he was sincere.

Ronald Reagan had clear and compelling beliefs, and he shared them in his messages and speeches. He believed in an America that was strong yet compassionate, courageous and just, hardworking and fair.

His were the core values of those who grew up in the Great Depression and took care of each other. His were the values of the "Greatest Generation," who fought in World War II to liberate the world from tyranny. His style of speaking was simple and clear: His speeches were no longer than 20 minutes and began by saying what he would say and then saying it. [41]

And Ronald Reagan ascended to the moral high ground when he stood in front of the Berlin Wall and challenged his Soviet counterpart, declaring, "General Secretary Gorbachev, if you seek peace, if you seek prosperity for the Soviet Union and Eastern Europe, if you seek liberalization: Come here to this gate! Mr. Gorbachev open this gate! Mr. Gorbachev, tear down this wall!

Reagan's ability to communicate reflected the inner person.
He believed that as an American he was living in the greatest country on earth and that it was each person's responsibility to be concerned about the welfare of their fellow man and woman.

He was once asked what he viewed as his utmost achieve-ment. His response defined him well.

He said that in the 1920s he was a lifeguard. In the span of seven summers, he saved 77 lives. He considered that his greatest accomplishment.[42]

As we express our gratitude, we must never forget that the highest appreciation is not to utter words, but to live by them.

Change is the law of life. And those who look only to the past or

President John F. Kennedy, courtesy of Library of Congress

present are certain to miss the future.

Let every nation know, whether it wishes us well or ill, that we shall pay any price, bear any burden, meet any hardship, support any friend, oppose any foe, in order to assure the survival and the success of liberty.

And so, my fellow Americans: ask not what your country can do for you — ask what you can do for your country.

— John F. Kennedy

---

[42] NPR, "The Life of Ronald Reagan: A TimeLine," September 18, 2015 (in 1926, Reagan begins work as a lifeguard at Lowell Park, near Dixon. He was credited with saving 77 lives during the seven summers he worked there) (http://www.npr.org/news/specials/obits/reagan/timeline.html)

John F. Kennedy: The Berlin Wall

John F. Kennedy delivering his speech at the Berlin Wall, courtesy of National Archives

John Kennedy combined personal charisma with ability to articulate ideas and transmit them with grace, charm, and strong oratorical skills. In "Profile of an Orator: John F. Kennedy," Brian Leggett described JFK's skill this way:[43]

Unlike Ronald Reagan or Margaret Thatcher who were conviction speakers with ideological messages, John Kennedy's platform was more inspiring, pragmatic, and liberal. His Inaugural Address and his speech at the Berlin Wall are examples of this. He was a man of his time, and his style suited this epoch of the mass media. Following the dull post war years of the Eisenhower administration, he brought a new spirit to the body politic. Kennedy's attractive non-verbal style did much to endear him to his audiences.

---

[43] Brian Leggett, "Profile of an Orator: John F. Kennedy," April 4, 2012, IESE Business School Journal in Spain, (http://blog.iese.edu/leggett/2012/04/12/profile-of-an-orator-john-f-kennedy/)

It was a windy and chilly day in Berlin. It was June 1963. President John F. Kennedy rose to speak. A multitude was waiting to hear his words. They would prove to be memorable and historic:

> *Freedom is indivisible, and when one man is enslaved, all are not free.*
> *When all are free, then we look — can look forward to that day when*
> *this city will be joined as one and this country and this great Continent*
> *of Europe in a peaceful and hopeful globe. When that day finally*
> *comes, as it will, the people of West Berlin can take sober satisfaction*
> *in the fact that they were in the front lines for almost two decades.*
> *... All free men, wherever they may live, are citizens of Berlin. And,*
> *therefore, as a free man, I take pride in the words, "Ich bin ein Berliner."*

John F. Kennedy had the talent to communicate a feeling that few of his generation could convey to a new generation of young people:

JFK's vision was not tangible. Kennedy conveyed feeling, under-standing, and that nothing was impossible.

President Franklin Delano Roosevelt, courtesy of Franklin Roosevelt Presidential Library

The only thing we have to fear is fear itself.

Human kindness has never weakened the stamina or softened the fiber of a free people. A nation does not have to be cruel to be tough.

Yesterday, December seventh, 1941, a date which will live in infamy, the United States of America was suddenly and deliberately attacked by naval and air forces of the Empire of Japan. We will gain the inevitable triumph, so help us God.
In the future days which we seek to make secure, we look forward to a world founded upon four essential human freedoms.

The first is freedom of speech and expression — everywhere in the world. The second is freedom of every person to worship God in his own way — everywhere in the world.

The third is freedom from want, which, translated into world terms, means economic understandings which will secure to every nation a healthy peacetime life for its inhabitants — everywhere in the world.

The fourth is freedom from fear, which, translated into world terms, means a world-wide reduction of armaments to such a point and in such a thorough fashion that no nation will be in a position to commit an act of physical aggression against any neighbor — anywhere in the world. That is no vision of a distant millennium. It is a definite basis for a kind of world attainable in our own time and generation.

There is a mysterious cycle in human events. To some generations, much is given. Of other generations, much is expected. This generation of Americans has a rendezvous with destiny.

— FDR

Franklin Delano Roosevelt: The Fireside Chats

When Franklin Roosevelt was inaugurated President in March 1933, he inherited from Herbert Hoover a nation that was facing the greatest economic downturn in U.S. history.

The American Great Depression became a global calamity that spread around the world. Millions of people lost their jobs, thousands of businesses and institutions disappeared. Roosevelt knew that the people needed hope. They needed to be told the government would take action to meet their needs.

The means he would use was the radio.

Radio was growing in popularity. Nearly every American home had one by 1933.

It allowed people to use their imaginations as they listened.
They could create their own images and ideas from the voices, the music, and sounds. This was a perfect medium for Franklin Delano Roosevelt.

His distinctive voice, his natural optimism and control, flowed over the airwaves into homes with his "Fireside Chats."
No one could see his disability.

All they could do was concentrate on his words, his ideas, and the feelings he conveyed.

President Franklin D. Roosevelt delivered his first fireside chat, on the banking crisis, eight days after taking office on March 12, 1933, courtesy of the Library of Congress

His broadcasts helped shape American history as never before. He won the hearts and minds of the voting public to support his programs. His speeches helped pass and implement the New Deal, and they helped harness the energy of the country to tackle the economic and social problems the nation faced.

His "Day of Infamy" speech on December 8, 1941, asking for a declaration of war against Japan, united the nation behind the government and brought the United States to victory.

Social Media and the Presidency

A Commander in Chief must be a splendid communicator and articulate solutions to earn trust, respect, and support from the people and the institutions that govern the nation.

He or she needs to know the importance and proper use of social media to convey messages, solicit feedback, and broaden and deepen the process of democratic inclusion so that more people comprehend our collective stake in a successful presidency.

Some thoughts about the use of social media and the current presidency are in order:

If someone is sitting in a restaurant, walking down the street, taking a seat on the bus, among countless other mundane activities, what is one glaring phenomenon they might observe? Beams of bright blue light illuminating the faces of Americans everywhere, providing unlimited digital assistance for an unfathomable number of tasks. Almost a decade ago, Apple Inc. trademarked the phrase of an era, "There's an app for that." Browse the App Store for weather forecasts, roadmaps, fitness trackers, mobile banking, video games, cameras, music, and movies, all simultaneously held in the palm of your hand. What about direct lines of communication to the most prominent of citizens, say, the President of the United States? There are apps for that, too.

In a world where information seekers are instantly gratified, should it be considered appropriate for a sitting U.S. President to have a personal social media platform? Although social networking allows for extreme transparency between the president and the people, during the time an individual holds the title of U.S. President, he or she should not update a personal social media platform, especially as it could potentially become a threat to national security.

At the end of the day, freedom of speech is a fundamental right for everyone in the country – even the president. Many might demand Trump to be more professional in his tweets, but he was elected by the people, and the people deserve to hear his thoughts. The difference between the "@POTUS" (President of the United States) Twitter account may be radically different between Obama and Trump, but we believe this change is good. The more transcendent the President and politicians are, then the more informed the people become. Trump's Twitter storms may scare some, but we believe this change will be for the better, in the end, as social media is truly one of the fastest, most unbiased ways to receive information from influential figures.[44]

Trump's presence as the first Twitter-based presidency is no fluke. His social media presence is intentional and strategic, his posts –

while individually senseless – are collectively incredibly shareable. This is what matters in politics in the Internet era, a candidate's ability to enter the household through televisions, computers, cell phones, and more. While it is difficult to view Trump as successful in the political realms that traditionally have shaped the presidency, his continued success is owed largely to his ability to navigate the modern globalized world. However the rest of his presidency develops, at least one aspect will remain constant: Trump's active online presence is not only definitive of his presidency, but no doubt will shape and inspire all subsequent national elections for as long as social media can reign supreme.[45]

I use social media as an idea generator, trend mapper and strategic compass.

— Paul Barron

We must get the American public to look past the glitter, beyond the showmanship, to the reality, the hard substance of things. And we will do it not so much with speeches that will bring people to their feet, as with speeches that bring people to their senses.

— Mario Cuomo

---

[44] (https://mediamilwaukee.com/top-stories/social-media-and-the-u-s-presidency)
[45] (https://www.diggitmagazine.com/articles/Trump-Twitter-Based-Presidency)

PART TWO: Leadership Qualities of The Commander in Chief
CHAPTER FOUR: ▬▬▬▬▬▬▬▬▬▬▬▬▬▬▬▬▬▬
The Brain Trust and the Understanding of Collaboration

Teamwork makes the dream work, but a vision becomes a nightmare when the leader has a big dream and a bad team.
— **John C. Maxwell**

Talent wins games, but teamwork and intelligence wins championships.
— **Michael Jordan**

You can talk about teamwork on a baseball team, but I'll tell you, it takes teamwork when you have 2,900 men stationed on the U.S.S. Alabama in the South Pacific.
— **Bob Feller**

Unity is strength... when there is teamwork and collaboration, wonderful things can be achieved.
— ***Mattie Stepanek***

We should seek by all means in our power to avoid war, by analyzing possible causes, by trying to remove them, by discussion in a spirit of collaboration and good will.

— **Neville Chamberlain**

America still has the right stuff to thrive. We still have the most creative, diverse, innovative culture and open society — in a world where the ability to imagine and generate new ideas with speed and to implement them through global collaboration is the most important competitive advantage.

— **Thomas Friedman**

The only thing that will redeem mankind is cooperation.

— **Bertrand Russell**

The ability of a president or a prime minister to succeed in tackling the enormous challenges that face a country depends on the people they bring into their government to govern with them and their ability to collaborate with them to get the job done and, of great importance, their skill in working with Congress or Parliament.

They cannot do it alone.

In the case of the United States, thousands of political appointees must be selected, cleared, and approved by the Senate, and put into place to oversee the vast bureaucracy of the American government. Our most successful presidents have brought with them a 'Brain Trust' of talent to help them lead. And they have worked closely with them to achieve their objectives.

The President of the United States confronts a wide range of issues that no chief executive of any other country deals with.

The president must be able to work with international leaders on a whole range of issues, from war to peace, from the environment to terrorism, and epidemics that cross global boundaries.

Among the president's most critical decisions is formation of a team to make the transition from candidate to president and who will lead the cabinet agencies.

The President's Cabinet

The Cabinet is the president's team.

The Secretary of each major department and the heads of each agency administer the apparatus of the government.

They also transmit the philosophy of the new administration.

The policies, plans, principles, and laws that the president wants to put into effect, with the approval of Congress, flow through the bureaucracy administered by his Cabinet.

Under each department and agency head are scores of offices with specific functions managed by political appointees. They reflect the principles of the administration.

They take the same oath as the President of the United States and swear to protect and defend the Constitution.

Those appointed to high political offices must have integrity, skill, and trust.

"When we elect a president, we elect a government."

The Cabinet of the President of the United States consists of:

Vice President
Secretary of State
Secretary of Treasury
Secretary of Defense
Attorney General (Justice Department Head)
Secretary of Interior
Secretary of Agriculture
Secretary of Commerce
Secretary of Labor
Secretary of Health & Human Services
Secretary of Housing & Urban Development
Secretary of Transportation
Secretary of Energy
Secretary of Education
Secretary of Veteran Affairs
Chief of Staff of the White House
Director of the Office of Management & Budget
Legal Counselor to the President
U.S. Trade Representative

FDR's Brain Trust

Time magazine did a study to examine the 10 best Cabinet members in the 20th Century. 4 of the 10 were members of President Franklin Roosevelt's Cabinet.[46]

The first 100 days of the Roosevelt administration were characterized by a whirlwind of activity by a group of advisers to the president known as the "Brain Trust."

Franklin D. Roosevelt's 1933 Brains Trust

| Adolf Berle | Raymond Moley | Rexford Tugwell |
| (1895–1971) | (1886–1975) | (1891–1979) |

Courtesy of Armstrong Economics (http://www.armstrongeconomics.com/research/economic-thought/economics/roosevelts-brains-trust)

---

[46] *Time*, November 13, 2008, "Top Ten Best Cabinet Members," (http://content.time.com/time/specials/packages/completelist/0,29569,1858368,00.html)

"Looks as if the new Leadership was really going to lead,"
March 7t, 1933, by Ray of the *Kansas City Star*

They were charged with taking action to solve the nation's severe economic problems and prepare legislation to move the government to tackle the poverty and pessimism of America's Great Depression.

FDR asked for emergency powers from Congress, and he immediately set about using them.

One of his first acts was to declare a bank holiday, which shut down every bank in the country, to stop depositors from withdrawing their money, which ended the nationwide panic.

The largest volume of legislation in U.S. history was passed in a matter of months. By 1938, the Franklin Roosevelt administration had transformed the American economy in a way that no one before or after him has done, through legislation that was called the "New Deal."[47]

---

[47] The Gilder Lehrman Institute of American History, New Deal Legislation

1932	Reconstruction Finance Corporation	Granted emergency loans to banks, life insurance companies, and railroads
1933	Civilian Conservation Corps (CCC)	Employed youth in reforestation, road construction, and flood control projects
	Agricultural Adjustment Act	Direct payments to farmers to reduce production
	Tennessee Valley Authority (TVA)	Creates independent public corporation to construct dams and power projects
	National Industrial Recovery Act	Establishes fair-competition codes; section 7a guarantees labor's right to organize Public Works Administration public works
1934	Federal Housing Administration (FHA)	Insured home loans
1935	Works Progress Administration (WPA)	Employed 8 million on public works projects
	Social Security Act	Established unemployment compensation and old age insurance
	National Labor Relations Act	Creates National Labor Relations Board to prevent unfair labor practices
1937	National Housing Act	Authorizes low rent public housing projects
1938	Fair Labor Standards Act	minimum wage of 40 cts/hr and 40-hour work week

The Cabinet of President Franklin Roosevelt, 1933, courtesy of the Library of Congress

Roosevelt appointed a cabinet that was skilled politically, economically, and socially.

It included the first woman, Francis Perkins, as Secretary of Labor. FDR relied on his Brain Trust to help create new laws and work legislation through Congress. His Cabinet ran the bureaucracy, interfacing with the House and Senate and the many related constituencies in business, labor, and farming.

FDR relied on Secretary Perkins and Eleanor Roosevelt to stay in close touch with social groups throughout the nation, to better understand and meet the needs of the people.

In a review of Ken Burn's PBS Documentary, "The Roosevelts," Professor Peter Drier says:[48]

---

[48] Peter Drier, George Mason University, "Ken Burns Overlooks the Secret of FDR's Success: The Power of the People," HNN History News Network, September 28, 2014 (http://historynewsnetwork.org/article/157061)

Burns and his interviewees describe FDR as courageous, bold, supremely self-confident, optimistic, not rigidly ideological, open to new ideas, and willing to experiment. In his actions and speeches (including his popular fireside chats on the radio), FDR gave Americans confidence in themselves and reminded them that the national government could be a positive force in their daily lives.

But missing from "The Roosevelts" is the real secret of FDR's success — the escalating protests that created a sense of urgency throughout the country and the political savvy of a small cadre of FDR's progressive advisors.

FDR may not have ended the Great Depression. Yet he provided hope and strength to the people of America that they could continue to grow and develop, even during difficult times.

He created stronger alliances between industry, labor, and agriculture through "priming the pump" to increase consumption, laws supporting workers' rights, and helping farmers rise up from the Dust Bowl.

Ray, the *Kansas City Star*, 1937

This coalition and the economic resiliency created by the New Deal prepared the generation that would confront America's greatest challenge to that point: World War II.

Saint-Memin sketched this last portrait of Washington in Philadelphia in November 1799 (John Hill Morgan, *Life Portraits of George Washington, and Their Replicas* [1931])

If the freedom of speech is taken away, then dumb and silent, we may be led, like sheep to the slaughter.

The Constitution is the guide which I never will abandon.

Observe good faith and justice toward all nations. Cultivate peace and harmony with all.... To be prepared for war is one of the most effective means of preserving peace.

I hope I shall possess firmness and virtue enough to maintain what I consider the most enviable of all titles, the character of an honest man.

My first wish is to see this plague of mankind, war, banished from the earth.

— George Washington

George Washington and the first "Team of Rivals"[49]

When Washington assumed the office of the President on April 30th, 1789, he found a nation with serious financial problems and, most of all, without the ability to carry out the principles in the Bill of Rights and the Constitution.

And it was his task to create the first government of the United States of America.

Washington picked men of courage and skill to be his advisers and the members of his Cabinet.

There were four (there are 16 today): Thomas Jefferson, Secretary of State; Alexander Hamilton, Secretary of Treasury; Henry Knox, Attorney General; and Edmond Randolph, Attorney General. President Washington trusted and relied on them to help construct the new republic on strong democratic principles.

Washington proved to be a wise and pragmatic visionary because he understood human nature. He knew Hamilton and Jefferson were serious political and philosophical rivals. Jefferson felt he represented the common man. Hamilton believed in the merchant class and the aristocracy.

Washington needed their brilliance to run the nascent government. He presided over their disputes, keep them in check, and delayed the beginning of party warfare.

He needed time to set his house in order and, in the process, stay out of Europe's deadly quarrels.

Washington felt that America required three decades of peace and prosperity before it could resist any aggression from foreign powers. He was right.

---

[49] In reference to the book, Team of Rivals, by Doris Kearns Goodwin, Simon and Shuster: New York, 2005

During his eight years in office, he proved to be a splendid administrator. He held regular Cabinet meetings, allowing his team to debate, but leaving the final decisions for himself. And he followed up to make sure those decisions were implemented. In sum, he knew how to delegate, control, and command.

George Washington was a superb judge of character and talent.

Washington and his 'brain trust' organized the Executive Branch, established the federal judiciary, helped amend the Constitution, and established the location of the nation's capital. He also created the first bank of the United States, established the dollar as the medium of exchange among the 13 states, started the U.S. Navy, and signed treaties of friendship with other countries.

Washington's influence lasted for decades and produced the foundation and values that helped grow the new country.

Lincoln presented the Emancipation Proclamation to his Cabinet on July 22, 1862. Shown from left to right are: Edwin M. Stanton, Secretary of War (seated); Salmon P. Chase, Secretary of the Treasury (standing); President Abraham Lincoln; Gideon Welles, Secretary of the Navy (seated); Caleb Blood Smith, Secretary of the Interior (standing); William H. Seward, Secretary of State (seated); Montgomery Blair, Postmaster General (standing); Edward Bates, Attorney General (seated); courtesy of the U.S. Senate

We need the strongest men of the party in the Cabinet. We needed to hold our own people together. I had looked the party over and concluded that these were the very strongest men. Then I had no right to deprive the country of their services.

— Abraham Lincoln

President Lincoln's Cabinet

No other president had encountered the trials of Abraham Lincoln. He entered the presidency with an empty treasury and with a country divided by slavery, which threatened the existence of the United States. He needed the best talent to help him, and he made sure he got it. Lincoln did not care if his Cabinet liked him or disagreed with him and each other, because he realized that it was he who bore the burden of ultimate responsibility.

They had a serious task before them: save the Union and end slavery. That was his two-pronged goal. He needed strong leaders to run the agencies and defeat the South in the Civil War.

1860 Republican Party Presidential Candidates, courtesy of National Archives

All his chief rivals for the Republican nomination for president in 1860 were part of his Cabinet: William H. Seward, Salmon P. Chase, Simon Cameron, and Edward Bates. The selection involved considerable conflict. Some were promised jobs as part of the deal to support Lincoln's nomination. Several objected to the inclusion of their rivals in the Cabinet. Disagreements arose about geographic distribution of jobs, balance between former members of the Democratic and Whig parties, differences on ideology and personality, and ethics. Cameron, for example, was attacked for his reputation of shady political and financial transactions.

But Lincoln saw the true value of his team members. For example, Seward, as Secretary of State, could be depended on to keep close ties with the British and the French to avoid having them take sides in the Civil War. Secretary of War Stanton was tough and determined and resilient, especially in the early years of the war, which were difficult for the North. Chase, as Secretary of the Treasury, was able to handle financing the war effort; he worked with Lincoln to create the greenback, which was the U.S.'s first universal paper currency, and found ways to raise funds to help win the conflict.

The members of Lincoln's Cabinet were fiercely independent, opinionated, and prone to constant conflict. They had one overriding factor in common: They were appointed by Abraham Lincoln. They respected him and his authority, even though this did not always seem the case.

Lincoln was supremely confident in his own ability to make wise choices after he listened to the opinions of his advisers. During Cabinet sessions and individual meetings with Cabinet officers, he would patiently concentrate on the discussion at hand, allow everyone their say, and then he would decide.

He was never in a hurry or showed impatience.

He was constantly cordial and pleasant to everyone.

He rarely revealed his thoughts until he made up his mind. At that point, it was clear that the last word was that of Abraham Lincoln.

Lincoln showed remarkable courage and wisdom in selecting a "team of rivals" for his Cabinet. If he had done otherwise, the outcome of the Civil War might have been quite different.

Abraham Lincoln also created the benchmarks of the modern presidency. His was the role model. His high character, integrity, perseverance, and wisdom unquestionably demonstrated that a president could succeed by being virtuous as well as skillful, focused, and determined to succeed.

A case where another president needed a strong 'brain trust' and Cabinet to help him and a powerful international coalition to deal with an international crisis was when George H.W. Bush had to confront the challenge of the Iraqi invasion of Kuwait in 1990.

"A new breeze is blowing, and a world refreshed by freedom seems reborn; for in man's heart, if not in fact, the day of the dictator is over. The totalitarian era is passing, its old ideas blown away like leaves from an ancient, lifeless tree.

"We do not want an America that is closed to the world. What we want is a world that is open to America.

"I can tell you this: If I am ever in a position to call the shots, I am not going to rush to send somebody else's kids into a war.

One of the good things about the way the Gulf War ended in 1991 is, you'd see the Vietnam veterans marching with the Gulf War veterans.

— George H. W. Bush

George H. W. Bush announcing the start of the first Gulf War, January 16, 1991,
courtesy of George Herbert Walker Bush Presidential Library

George H. W. Bush's International Coalition in the Gulf War

"Just 2 hours ago, allied air forces began an attack on military targets in Iraq and Kuwait. These attacks continue as I speak. Ground forces are not engaged.

"This conflict started August 2nd when the dictator of Iraq invaded a small and helpless neighbor. Kuwait — a member of the Arab League and a member of the United Nations — was crushed, its people brutalized. Five months ago, Saddam Hussein started this cruel war against Kuwait. Tonight, the battle has been joined."[50]

With these words, President George H. W. Bush announced the start of the battle to liberate Kuwait from the grip of Saddam Hussein. Five months earlier, Iraq invaded Kuwait. The aggression sent shock waves around the world.

President George H. W. Bush saw the attack as a threat to the economic and global political interests of the United States. It was also a threat to the oil states in the Persian Gulf, and it was a direct threat to the international system that was evolving after the end of the Cold War.

---

[50] The History Place, Great Speeches Collection, "G.H.W. Bush Announcing War Against Iraq" (http://www.history-place.com/speeches/bush-war.htm)

Bush believed that reversing the conquest of Kuwait would help create a "new world order" to prevent this kind of action happening in the future. He equated the invasion in terms of "good and evil," comparing Saddam Hussein to Adolf Hitler.

"Iraq's era under President Saddam Hussein was notorious for its severe violations of human rights, which were perceived to be among the worst, if not the worst, in the world. Secret police, state terrorism, torture, mass murder, genocide, ethnic cleansing, rape, deportations, extrajudicial killings, forced disappearances, assassinations, chemical warfare, and the destruction of southern Iraq's marshes were some of the methods Saddam and the country's Ba'athist government used to maintain control. The total number of deaths related to torture and murder during this period is unknown, but estimated to be around 250,000, according to Human Rights Watch, with the great majority of those occurring as a result of the 1988 Anfal genocide and the suppression of the 1991 uprisings in Iraq. Human Rights Watch and Amnesty International issued regular reports of widespread imprisonment and torture."[51]

Coalition forces from France, Kuwait, Syria, Oman, and Egypt assemble during Operation Desert Storm, courtesy of the U.S. Department of the Navy

[51] (https://en.wikipedia.org/wiki/Human_rights_in_Saddam_Hussein%27s_Iraq)

Within hours of the introduction of the U.S. proposal, the United Nations Security Council passed the first of twelve resolutions condemning Iraq and imposing sanctions. Even the Soviet Union stood by the U.S., condemning Iraq's invasion of Kuwait and halting arm sales to Iraq. The United States fought the war to liberate Kuwait with a coalition of international forces.

President Bush was directly involved in planning the war effort. He wanted a clear-cut victory that was quick and decisive and left no room for defeat. A day after his speech, allied and American forces started air attacks on Iraqi forces. Thirty-seven days later, the ground campaign began. Exactly one hundred hours after the start of the campaign, the coalition announced, "Mission accomplished." Iraqi invasion forces were driven out of Kuwait.

The day will come — and it is not far off — when the legacy of Lincoln will finally be fulfilled at 1600 Pennsylvania Avenue, when a black man or woman will sit in the Oval Office. When that day comes, the most remarkable thing about it will be how naturally it occurs.

— George H. W. Bush

The Ability to Work with the Congress

I don't make jokes. I just watch the government and report the facts.

Ancient Rome declined because it had a Senate, now what is going to happen to us with both a House and a Senate?

I am not a member of any organized political party. I am a Democrat.

— Will Rogers

The Congress can be an ally or an enemy to a new administration.

It is up to the president to have the skill, patience, and wherewithal to understand how to work closely with the House and the Senate. Our most effective presidents have been able to deal with Congress, even when both houses were in opposition. Several presidents enjoyed majorities in the Congress, which gave them significant opportunities to change the course of events.

For example, in the last century, three Chief Executives stand out in their ability to control and sway the Congress and pass important legislation: Woodrow Wilson, Franklin Roosevelt, and Lyndon Johnson.

Woodrow Wilson being sworn in on March 4, 1913, courtesy of Library of Congress

Woodrow Wilson's "New Freedom"

Woodrow Wilson entered the presidency in 1913 with a strong sense of purpose and aggressiveness.[52] He believed the presidency was a place "in which a man must put on war paint."

---

[52] August Heckscher, Woodrow Wilson, Easton Press, 1991, pp. 265-267

Wilson was bold and willing to gamble for great stakes to achieve his goals. He approached politics this way from winning the governorship of New Jersey in 1911 and then to become the 28th President of the United States two years later. He defeated the incumbent Republican president, William Howard Taft, and one of the most popular politicians in American history, Theodore Roosevelt, in a three-party race.

Wilson was the first Southerner elected to the Presidency since 1869. He campaigned as a reformer and advocate of control over big business and political patronage. He enjoyed a Democratic majority in the Congress. As a college professor, Wilson had studied and written about politics, the party system, and the Congress. He was a keen student of how the apparatus worked and used his knowledge to push his "New Freedom" program to create the Federal Reserve, the Federal Trade Commission, the enactment of a progressive income tax, and stronger anti-trust measures.

He skillfully manipulated the Democratic caucus to carefully coordinate with Congressional leaders to introduce and pass his legislation. Often, Republicans were kept out of conference committee deliberations and left out of the legislative process. "Never did the lash of the presidential and caucus whip cut so deep as today," one Republican complained.[53]

By the end of World War I in 1918, the legislative situation had changed. The Senate was now in the hands of Republicans. And they remembered Wilson's style of ramming through laws with little or no consultation. Also, Wilson did not invite members of the opposition to join him at the Paris Peace Conference in Versailles. Republicans did not forget this. When he returned from the conference, President Wilson wanted the Senate to accept the offer to join the League of Nations.

He refused to compromise, even when the Republicans introduced amendments that were deemed acceptable. The proposal was defeated. It was an historic mistake on the part of the Executive and Legislative branches of our government. Historians claim that if the U.S. had been an active member of the League, many of the events leading up to World War II could have been avoided.

---

[53] "How Presidents Work Congress," by Julian E. Zelizer, *Politico*, July 27, 2009 (http://www.politico.com/story/2009/07/how-presidents-work-congress-025441#ixzz3qzAyXNTM)

The question of the League and the comportment of President Wilson during the Paris Peace Conference brings into question a serious issue about the U.S. presidency: the health of the president.

The first ominous signs of President Wilson's serious health issues showed up in the summer of 1918, when the he began to suffer from severe breathing problems. The issue was hushed up, but it was the prelude to more critical problems to come. Historian John Milton Cooper, a Wilson scholar at the University of Wisconsin, in his 2001 book, *Breaking the Heart of the World: Woodrow Wilson and the Fight for the League of Nations*, claimed that President Wilson was not well in Paris. He was under considerable psychological and physical stress, so much so that it may have affected his ability to negotiate and come to grips with the realities of the post-war period in Europe.[54]

Returning to America, Wilson set out on a demanding public speaking tour to gain support for ratification of the Treaty of Versailles and the proposal for American membership in the League of Nations. On September 25, 1919, President Wilson collapsed while in Pueblo, Colorado. He never fully recovered.

Two weeks later, he suffered a serious stroke. Wilson was paralyzed on the left side and partially blind. He remained bed ridden for weeks. His wife arranged for him to have absolute privacy and keep his condition from reaching the public until February 1920, when it became known. He remained in seclusion for the rest of his time in office. "This is the worst instance of presidential disability we've ever had," according to John Milton Cooper. "We stumbled along . . . without a fully functioning President" for a year and a half, he said.[55]

Woodrow Wilson died on February 3, 1924, at the age of sixty-seven. Wilson's fitness for the presidency was questioned during and after his time in office. It became an issue that was part of the motivation

---

[54] John Milton Cooper, *Breaking the Heart of the World: Woodrow Wilson and the Fight for the League of Nations*, Cambridge University Press: London, 2001

[55] Michael Alison Chandler, "A President's Illness Kept Under Wraps," *Washington Post* Staff Writer, Saturday, February 3, 2007

to pass the 25th Amendment to the Constitution in 1967, which dealt with the succession to the presidency if the incumbent were unable to discharge his or her duties or resign.

FDR and the Congress

It IS a New Deal

"It IS a New Deal," March 11, 1933, by Talburt in the *Pittsburgh Press*, courtesy FDR Library

The election of 1932 gave Franklin Roosevelt a majority of Democrats in Congress. He got 57% of the vote, while his party went from 50% of the seats in the House of Representatives to 72%. The Democrats also dominated the Senate, with 59 Senators.

Two years later, his majority grew. It was the election of 1934 that gave FDR the Congress he needed to enact most of the legislation of the New Deal.

FDR seemed unstoppable. He dominated Congress and its activities during his first term and, with the landslide election of 1934, he placed his party in a dominant position for the first time since the 1850s. Roosevelt campaigned extensively for congressional candidates.

Many owed their careers to him. With his massive re-election mandate of 1936, Roosevelt and Congress believed that the people wanted to continue the policies of the New Deal, to re-engineer the economic and social conditions of America.

"During his first two terms, FDR oversaw some of the most far-reaching economic and social legislation in the nation's history, including Social Security, protections of workers' rights to unionize, a federal minimum wage, heavier taxes on the wealthy, new regulations on banks, public utilities and business stock transactions, a huge work relief program for the unemployed, and unemployment insurance. Several government-sponsored enterprises brought electricity and jobs to rural areas, including the Tennessee Valley Authority. The Civilian Conservation Corps put 300,000 young men to work in 1,200 camps planting trees, building bridges, and cleaning beaches. The Public Works Administration (PWA), and later the Works Progress Administration (WPA), provided jobs to millions of Americans to build schools, libraries, hospitals, airports, and roads. It also paid artists, writers, actors and others to create murals, produce plays and musicals, and write travel guides and oral histories."[56]

That alliance of FDR and Congress changed the face of the United States forever.

Lyndon Baines Johnson: Man of the Congress

Lyndon Baines Johnson, 1964, courtesy of National Archives

The Democratic Party won seven out of nine presidential elections from 1932 to 1964. During those three decades, they enjoyed almost a continuous majority in the Congress. Lyndon Johnson rose in the ranks of the party, beginning in the second administration of FDR. He became a member of the House in 1937 and served until 1949, when he was elected Senator from his home state of Texas.

For the next dozen years, Johnson rose in the ranks to become one of the most powerful Senate majority leaders in history. He was sworn in as Vice President in 1961 and became President with the assassination of John F. Kennedy.

The distinguishing characteristic of Johnson that separated him from other presidents was his profound roots in the Congress. After serving more than 20 years, he became an expert in moving legislation through both houses. He could cajole or intimidate and convince his colleagues to support his positions. He was quite resourceful, but also willing to compromise. And he carried this well-honed skill into the White House.

LBJ was elected in 1964 with over 61% of the vote, which was the highest vote-share up to that time. The Democrats won the largest majorities in Congress since FDR's election of 1936. Johnson set about passing the program advocated by President Kennedy and creating welfare legislation for what he coined, "The War on Poverty." Thanks to his strong control of the legislative branch, he was able to pass a flurry of laws that were comparable to those of the New Deal in terms of impact on society and the economy. The laws included:

- 1963: Clean Air Act of 1963
- 1963: Higher Education Facilities Act of 1963
- 1963: Vocational Education Act of 1963
- 1964: Civil Rights Act of 1964
- 1964: Urban Mass Transportation Act of 1964
- 1964: Wilderness Act
- 1964: Nurse Training Act of 1964
- 1964: Food Stamp Act of 1964
- 1964: Economic Opportunity Act
- 1964: Housing Act of 1964[262]

- 1965: Higher Education Act of 1965
- 1965: Older Americans Act
- 1965: Coinage Act of 1965
- 1965: Social Security Act of 1965
- 1965: Voting Rights Act
- 1965: Immigration and Nationality Services Act of 1965
- 1966: Animal Welfare Act of 1966
- 1966: Freedom of Information Act (FOIA)
- 1967: Age Discrimination in Employment Act
- 1967: Public Broadcasting Act of 1967
- 1968: Architectural Barriers Act of 1968
- 1968: Bilingual Education Act
- 1968: Civil Rights Act of 1968
- 1968: Gun Control Act of 1968

Even the development of the FCC emergency number, 911, was created during the Johnson administration.

The same congress that helped Lyndon Johnson create "The Great Society" was also responsible for our involvement in Vietnam. Johnson's legacy as president and the legacy of the legislation he passed was summed up by the Miller Center of the University of Virginia:

"Johnson's administration passed an unprecedented amount of legislation, with much of it designed to protect the nation's land, air, water, wilderness, and quality of life—to keep Americans safer and the United States from becoming uglier and dirtier. President Johnson's administration also extended the New Deal of Franklin Roosevelt, including aid to education, Head Start, Medicare, and Medicaid—programs that are still significant today and that command bipartisan support for their effectiveness. But many of his initiatives for the arts, for the environment, for poverty, for racial justice, and for workplace safety angered many economic and social conservatives and became the targets of alienated white voters and tax revolters. The reaction to his Great Society and to broader trends helped spawn a dramatic political polarization in the United States that some historians have labeled a conservative counterrevolution.

"Further clouding Johnson's legacy was the devastating outcome of the Vietnam War. While his programs kept untold numbers of Americans out of poverty, gave others basic health care, and ensured the fundamental rights of citizenship for minorities, in Southeast Asia millions of Vietnamese lost their lives and homes, more than 58,000 American military personnel lost their lives, and hundreds of thousands more would have their lives permanently altered. At a time when Americans were reshaping the locus of power at home, events in Vietnam were raising serious questions about how America should use its clout abroad. The legacies of death, renewal, and opportunity attached to the Johnson administration are ironic, confusing, and uncertain. They will likely remain that way."[57]

Now more than ever we need leaders of democracies who will be able to identify and convince the best and brightest experts to join the government to tackle the great issues we confront.

A presidential 'brain trust' requires skill to build it and to manage a team dedicated to the principles that put them into office with the trust given them by the people.

Working closely with Congress and Parliament is essential.

No president or prime minister can govern with Executive Orders alone. They must work and collaborate with other nations to seek global peace and stability, especially today, when we face threats that risk the future of the safety and security of the entire planet.

---

[57] Miller Center, University of Virginia, "Lyndon B. Johnson: Impact and Legacy" (http://millercenter.org/president/biography/lbjohnson-impact-and-legacy)

PART TWO: Leadership Qualities of The Commander in Chief
CHAPTER FIVE:
Character, integrity, ethical behavior, and trustworthiness

Reputation is the shadow. Character is the tree.
— Abraham Lincoln

Goodness is about character — integrity, honesty, kindness, generosity, moral courage, and the like. More than anything else, it is about how we treat other people. — *Dennis Prager*

Character cannot be developed in ease and quiet. Only through experience of trial and suffering can the soul be strengthened, ambition inspired, and success achieved.
— Helen Keller

I have a dream that my four little children will one day live in a nation where they will not be judged by the color of their skin, but by the content of their character. — *Martin Luther King, Jr.*

Be more concerned with your character than your reputation, because your character is what you really are, while your reputation is merely what others think you are.
— John Wooden

In any moment of decision, the best thing you can do is the right thing, the next best thing is the wrong thing, and the worst thing you can do is nothing....I am really sorry for Taft... I am sure he means well, but he means well feebly, and he does not know how! He is utterly unfit for leadership and this is a time when we need leadership...No man is worth his salt who is not ready at all times to risk his well-being, to risk his body, to risk his life, in a great cause.
— Theodore Roosevelt

Theodore Roosevelt shortly before being shot, October 14 , 1912, courtesy of Library of Congress

The complex ethical features of each person govern the way we react in any situation. We call this Character.

It includes honesty, ethics, trustworthiness, and self-control.

It is about always doing the right thing, no matter what.

Someone, for instance, who has a character trait of straightforwardness and truthfulness, is more likely to report the facts than one who is prone to being deceptive.

A leader who is reliable, direct, and respects diversity will be more successful than one who misleads and lacks trust in others.

They accept the different qualities people have and appreciate them as an opportunity, and not as a problem.

Character stresses ethical behavior. It is the most important quality the Commander in Chief must have.

Without character, he or she would not be able to gain the loyalty of a team, of allies, and of the people they govern.

President William Howard Taft, courtesy of the White House

I am going to do what I think is best for the country, within my jurisdiction and power, and then let the rest take care of itself.

A man never knows exactly how the child of his brain will strike other people.

— William Howard Taft

Theodore Roosevelt: Attempted Assassination

It was 1912, and Republican William Howard Taft was running for re-election. He was up against the Democratic nominee, New Jersey Governor Woodrow Wilson, and one of the most popular men in American history, his former friend and mentor, Theodore Roosevelt.

Teddy occupied the Oval Office from 1901 to 1908. He refused to run for a third term to honor the precedent set by George Washington. He left the White House with soaring popularity as he turned over the reins to Taft.

Teddy went off to big game hunting in Africa to bring back specimens for the Smithsonian Institution.

He returned three years later.

| Governor of New York | Vice President | President | Peacemaker | Mighty Hunter all the time |

By then, Teddy had become dissatisfied with the performance of his successor.

He ran against Taft for the Republican nomination and far outpolled him in the primaries. Taft worked vigorously to control the party's organizational apparatus that ran the nomination process. The Republican National Convention selected him on June 22, 1912, as their standard bearer. Teddy's supporters met the next day to create a third party.

In August 1912, the newly formed Progressive Party convened with great enthusiasm.

Jane Adams, the legendary suffragette, gave a strong supporting speech to second the nomination of Theodore Roosevelt as the candidate for President of the United States of the Progressive Party (reporters coined it the Bull Moose Party in honor of Teddy).

He was selected by acclamation.

The platform was a detailed document of dramatic social change called "A Contract with the People." The theme was to eliminate the corrupt domination of business interests in politics.

It promised strict limits on campaign contributions, full disclosure of donations, and registration of lobbyists. The Social Platform called for a National Health Service, social insurance to provide for the disabled and elderly, and sweeping legislation for workers' rights, including a minimum wage for women and an eight-hour day.

Political reforms emphasized women's suffrage, recall elections, judicial recall, referendums, and the direct election of Senators.

Teddy carried out a vigorous campaign. He travelled extensively and gave scores of speeches and interviews. He met with people of all political persuasions and explained the principles of the Progressive Party Platform.

Roosevelt mixing spicy ingredients in his speeches in this 1912 editorial cartoon by Karl K. Knecht in the Evansville Courier, courtesy of Library of Congress

Theodore Roosevelt, courtesy of Library of Congress

On October 14, 1912, TR was campaigning in Milwaukee, Wisconsin. It was just after 8 PM when Roosevelt entered his car outside the Gilpatrick Hotel.

He rose and waved his hat to the crowd that gathered to greet him. Suddenly, a light flashed and an explosion lit the night air. A would-be assassin had shot Theodore Roosevelt at close range.

The bullet lodged against his rib on a path to his heart. It was slowed by an eyeglass case and his 50-page speech that he was on his way to give at the Milwaukee Auditorium.

The crowd now became a mob. The coolest head was that of Theodore Roosevelt. The man who entered the White House after the murder of William McKinley bellowed, "Don't hurt him. Bring him here." He asked, "What did you do it for?" The would-be assassin was silent. "Oh, what's the use? Turn him over to the police," said Teddy.

There were no signs of blood on his clothes. Roosevelt reached inside and felt a bullet hole, the size of a dime, on the right side in the lower part of his chest. He coughed three times to see if the bullet had penetrated his lung. It had not. A doctor accompanying the former president's caravan ordered the driver to go directly to the nearest hospital.

Roosevelt yelled, "No. You get me to that speech."[58]

Roosevelt told the audience he had been shot. The audience gasped.

It was a bombshell.

---

[58] David Kerisy and Ray Choiniere, Presidential Temperament: The Unfolding of Character in the Forty Presidents of the United States, University of Toronto Press: Toronto, 1992, Introduction

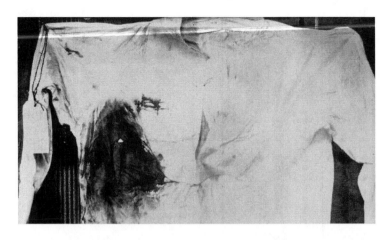

The "Bloody Shirt" of Theodore Roosevelt, Courtesy Library of Congress

He opened his vest and revealed his shirt, soaked in blood, and he took out his speech, which clearly had a bullet hole in it.

> *Fortunately, I had my manuscript, so you see I was going to make a long speech, and there is a bullet—there is where the bullet went through—and it probably saved me from it going into my heart. The bullet is in me now, so that I cannot make a very long speech, but I will try my best...I have a message to deliver," he declared to the stunned audience, "and I will deliver it as long as there is life in my body." It was a rousing performance. Roosevelt was a wonderful, charismatic orator under any circumstance, and the sight of his spattered shirt and notes added a spectacular portion of drama to his speech.*[59]

He continued his speech for 90 minutes.

Only then did he agree to go to the hospital. The bullet stayed with him for the rest of his life and exacerbated his chronic rheumatoid arthritis. A few weeks later, the votes were cast. Teddy drew over 4 million votes. It was 27% of the total, but fell behind Wilson, with 42%. Taft got only 23%.[60]

---

[59] Ibid. Kerisy and Choiniere
[60] Congressional Quarterly's Guide to U. S. elections, Washington, DC: Congressional Quarterly Inc., 1985, pp. 75, 387–388, ISBN 0-87187-339-, pp. 295, 348

"More Rough Riding," Teddy trying to dominate the Party, 1912 editorial cartoon by Karl K. Knecht in the Evansville Courier, courtesy of Library of Congress

"Two Gentlemen," Charles J. Budd, courtesy of *Harper's Weekly,* November 9, 1912

On March 4, 1913, Woodrow Wilson was sworn in as the 28th President of the United States, succeeding William Howard Taft.

"More Rough Riding," Teddy trying to dominate the Party, 1912 editorial cartoon
by Karl K. Knecht in the Evansville Courier, courtesy of Library of Congress

His kindly nature and lovable traits of character, and his amiable consideration for all about him will long live in the minds and hearts of his countrymen.

— Former President Grover Cleveland on the death of William McKinley

That is all a man can hope for during his lifetime — to set an example — and when he is dead, to be an inspiration for history.

— William McKinley

The Altruism of William McKinley

Eleven years before the attempt on Roosevelt's life, President William McKinley was also the victim of a gunman. McKinley was attending an event in Buffalo, New York, on September 6, 1901, when he was shot by an anarchist. The president died 8 days later. Theodore Roosevelt was sworn in on September 14, 1901.

The details of McKinley's shooting were almost identical to Roosevelt's: A famous political figure is walking in public; a lone madman steps up and fires a pistol point blank into his chest; the gunman is immediately wrestled to the ground while the bloodied victim, still conscious, sees his assailant subdued. In President McKinley's case, however, the rest of the story is quite different. As the mortally wounded McKinley watched the madman Leon Czolgosz being subdued, he cried out, "Don't let them hurt him!" Then, to his secretary, George Cortelyou, he gasped, "My wife—be careful, Cortelyou, how you tell her—oh, be careful!" Then, as his supporters rushed him to the hospital, he sighed, "It must have been some poor misguided fellow.[61]

The reaction of each man to the crisis in question revealed much about his character.

Teddy responded like the tough, fierce warrior he had been all his life. William McKinley, instead, while being a dedicated and determined leader, was by nature more considerate and gentler.

His first concern was the welfare of his assassin and the impact on his wife. This was typical of McKinley. Both men reacted to the same event in manners consistent with the way they lived and their personality: McKinley was a kind and serious caretaker; Teddy was a spur of the moment, enthusiastic swashbuckler.[62]

We are not suggesting here that social background and personal history are unimportant. Far from it; our social context stamps us inevitably and indelibly. But we feel quite safe in proposing that our lifelong patterns of action, our character, will always arise from and be consistent with our temperament. Thus, William McKinley and Teddy Roosevelt, each of a different temperament, could never have developed similar characters, similar ways of looking at and responding to the world.

---

[61] Ibid. Kerisy and Choiniere
[62] Ibid. Kerisy and Choiniere

They saw differently and they responded differently, quite consistently with their differing temperaments, even to the almost identical traumas of their shootings.[63]

Presidential Temperaments

David Kerisy and Ray Choiniere, in their 1992 book, *Presidential Temperament: The Unfolding of Character in the Forty Presidents of the United States*, studied the behavior of forty American presidents. They found that each acted in an amazing variety of ways.

Some were timid; some were vigorous; others were heroic and domineering figures, while others seemed immobile. At times, they took on the characteristics of animals. At times, they could be lions, exhibiting courage and strength; and other times, like foxes, acting with cunning and opportunism. They could be playful like dogs or beavers building and protecting their nests, or owls, high above all, waiting for a moment worthy of their attention.[64]

Kerisy and Choiniere explained the four basic temperaments from which the character of American presidents seem to be fashioned: Guardian, Idealists, Artisans, and Rational: [65]

Guardian

These types are considered "Concrete Cooperators," who dwell on their responsibilities and duties. They are protectors of what they can control and are careful to follow rules, respect the rights of others, and obey laws. "William McKinley is an example of the steadfast Guardian temperament and joins the distinguished company of American Presidents like George Washington, Grover Cleveland, and Harry Truman, all sober and serious men."[66]

---

[63] Ibid. Kerisy and Choiniere
[65] (http://www.keirsey.com/4temps/overview_temperaments.asp)
[66] Ibid. Keirsey

Idealists

These are considered as "Abstract Cooperators," who speak of hope and possibilities and try to act in good conscience and reach goals without compromising their ethics. Keirsey and Choiniere were unable to find any Presidents they considered to be "idealists." As examples, the closest leaders of this type from around the world would be Eleanor Roosevelt and Mahatma Gandhi.

Artisans

Such types are "Concrete Utilitarians," who deal in what they can see and touch and will act according to whatever will work, what results in an immediate payoff, even if rules must be twisted. Presidents in this category are daring, colorful, and charming, with charisma like Teddy Roosevelt, Andrew Jackson, John F. Kennedy, Lyndon Johnson, and Ronald Reagan.

Rational

These types are "abstract utilitarians," who speak about new challenges and new solutions. They are pragmatic and efficient and will ignore conventions and rules if necessary to get the job done. "Rational" has given us some of our most far-sighted and controversial Presidents, men of theory and strategy, such as Thomas Jefferson, James Madison, and Abraham Lincoln."[67]

According to Kerisey and Choiniere, Presidents are born with a certain temperament that has more bearing on their behavior than their background, education, social status, economic conditions, and the general conditions of their times.

Most biographers dwell on achievements and the era in which a President lives. Instead, temperament is a major factor in how they act

---

[67] Ibid. Keirsey

and what they do.

"Something is missed when the qualities of the seed and the tree, of temperament and character, are overlooked."[68]

President Dwight David Eisenhower, courtesy of Library of Congress

The most important point is that it is character that separates leaders who even have similar backgrounds. Truman, Eisenhower, and Lyndon Johnson came from rural upbringings and struggled in families that could barely make ends meet.

President Harry Truman after winning the 1948 election, courtesy of Library of Congress

[68] Ibid. Keirsey

The Their temperaments governed their time in the White House: Johnson had an Artisan temperament, Truman a Guardian temperament, and Eisenhower exhibited a Rational temperament.

Those who came from a patrician background demonstrated similar differences: John Kennedy (Artisan), Jimmy Carter (Guardian), and Thomas Jefferson (Rational).

Johnson, for instance, was often cunning and quite different from Eisenhower, who was self-controlled. JFK was stylish, while Carter was moralistic. Each could relate to one another in terms of disposition: JFK could understand LBJ, and they could take each other's measure. Eisenhower could appreciate an aristocratic Jefferson, a designer of buildings who created the University of Virginia.

Character, as a result, involves a lifelong pattern of behavior. As we have seen, once we determine the temperament of a President, we can forecast their behavior, to some extent. Their actions areed in families that could barely make ends meet. spontaneous parts of their predisposition to perform in certain ways.

"Thus, the innately vigorous Artisan Teddy Roosevelt could rejoice, 'A President has a great chance; his position is that of a king and a prime minister rolled into one,' and his habitual behavior would consistently reflect this dynamic Artisan perspective."[69]

President Calvin Coolidge, courtesy of Library of Congress

---

[69] Ibid. Keirsey

Calvin Coolidge: Example of A Guardian President

Calvin Coolidge was a perfect example of the Guardian temperament. He entered the White House in 1921 as Vice President, and left it as the President.

President Warren G. Harding died in San Francisco in August 1923, while Vice President Coolidge was with his father and family in the family farmhouse in Vermont. Coolidge showed his qualities as a person and leader when he recalled that momentous night in his memoirs: "On the night of August 2, 1923, I was awakened by my father coming up the stairs, calling my name. I noticed that his voice trembled. As the only times I had ever observed that before were when death had visited our family, I knew that something of the gravest nature had occurred. He placed in my hands an official report and told me that President Harding had just died. My wife and I at once dressed.

"Before leaving the room I knelt down and, with the same prayer with which I have since approached the altar of the church, asked God to bless the American people and give me power to serve them.
"My first thought was to express my sympathy for those who had been bereaved, and after that was done, to attempt to reassure the country with the knowledge that I proposed no sweeping displacement of the men then in office and that there were to be no violent changes in the administration of affairs. As soon as I had dispatched a telegram to Mrs. Harding, I therefore issued a short public statement declaratory of that purpose."[70]

Coolidge was a cautious and pessimistic President who protected his territory, the United States of America. He was concerned with its welfare and future. It was natural for him to warn the nation in 1928 that, even though it was enjoying prosperity, all could be easily lost.

---

[70] (https://www.senate.gov/about/officers-staff/vice-president/VP_Calvin_Coolidge.htm)

Calvin Coolidge being sworn in as President of the United States by a Notary Public on
August 2, 1923, on the death of President Warren G. Harding, Courtesy of the Library of Congress

A year later, the Wall Street Crash of 1929 happened. By then, Herbert
Hoover was in office.

In the same manner, it was natural for Thomas Jefferson to be a
visionary and long-range planner. "So, Jefferson could declare that the
United States was not merely another nation, but an 'experiment to
show whether man can be trusted with self-government.'"[71]

Maine Senator Edmond Muskie, courtesy of the U.S. Senate

---

[71] Ibid. Keirsey

The Fall of Edmond Muskie

One of the leading candidates for the nomination of the Democratic Party in the 1972 Presidential campaign was Maine Senator Edmond Muskie. He was considered a man of character and integrity. He was a victim of a "dirty trick" committed by Kenneth W. Clawson, a political aid of President Richard Nixon. Muskie was viewed as a strong challenger to Nixon's chances of reelection.

Courtesy of Pat Oliphant and the Susan Conway Gallery of Washington, DC

Throughout the New Hampshire campaign, the Manchester *Union Leader* attacked him. In an anonymous letter, he was accused of using the pejorative term "Canuck" in referring to the state's French Canadians. It was later discovered that Clawson had sent the letter to discredit Muskie. The paper also published an article accusing Muskie's wife of "unladylike" behavior. Muskie cracked.

A week before the New Hampshire primary, he hired a flatbed truck and stood before the *Union Leader* building in the snow. He passionately defended his wife and criticized the publisher and his paper. He then began to weep, according to some reporters. Muskie won the primary, but his poll numbers began to fall. He left the race six weeks after the campaign had begun.

The Senator's temperament was challenged. It was clear that he was a man of integrity, but doubts rose about his ability to control himself under pressure. He later said he had choked up over his anger. "It changed people's minds about me," he said about the incident. "They were looking for a strong, steady man, and here I was weak."[72]

Vice President Spiro Agnew, courtesy of the Office of the Vice President

The Resignation of Spiro Agnew

In the case of Spiro Agnew, Vice President under Richard Nixon, his character was challenged by an incident that happened as Governor of Maryland. He was accused of taking bribes in the form of campaign contributions from companies that won state contracts.

---

[72] (https://www.washingtonpost.com/wp-srv/politics/special/clinton/frenzy/muskie.htm)

Spiro Agnew Political Cartoon, courtesy of DeSoto, 1973

By 1973, President Nixon was facing impeachment for the Watergate cover up. The prospect of a simultaneous impeachment of the Vice President and President was real. Agnew pleaded "nolo contendere" to the charges against him, which meant that he acknowledged his guilt. He paid $160,000 for back taxes plus a $10,000 fine and was spared going to jail.

On October 10, 1973, he became the second Vice President to resign from office. (In 1832, John C. Calhoun left the Vice Presidency to take a Senate seat.) Agnew quit in the face of criminal charges of tax evasion and bribery of a public official.[73] Later, he was disbarred from the State of Maryland, calling him "morally obtuse."[74]

---

[73] Spiro T. Agnew, Go Quietly....or else, William Morrow, New York, 1980, p. 15.
[74] ABA Journal, May 2009 (http://www.abajournal.com/magazine/article/may_2_1974/)

President Gerald Ford, courtesy of Library of Congress

Gerald Ford: Vice President

Agnew was succeeded by Gerald Ford, Republican House Minority leader and a man with a reputation of honesty and character. James Cannon described the selection this way: [75]

Gerald R. Ford became President not because he was popular with the American public, not because he campaigned for the job, but because of his character.

More than any other president of this century, Ford was chosen for his integrity and trustworthiness; his peers in Congress put him in the White House because he told the truth and kept his word... Ford personified what Nixon was not. Ford was honest. He could be trusted. Throughout twenty-five years in the House of Representatives, Ford had proved himself to be a man of integrity. It was for that integrity that the highest powers of Congress, Democratic and Republican, chose Ford to be Vice President, knowing that Nixon's presidency was doomed......

---

[75] Cannon, James, "Character Above All" (http://www.pbs.org/newshour/spc/character/essays/ford.html)

President Richard Nixon announces the release of the Watergate Tapes,
April 29, 1974, courtesy of National Archives

Richard Nixon: Watergate

The Watergate scandal was one of the biggest in U.S. history involving a sitting president.

In 1972, five men were caught breaking into Democrat National Party Headquarters. A subsequent investigation discovered that Richard Nixon attempted to cover up information about the affair. The scandal grew, costing Nixon much of his political support. He resigned on August 9, 1974, in the face of possible impeachment and removal from office.

The incident revealed much about Nixon's character.

Nixon appeared cunning, secretive, and paranoiac. He was accused of using the Office of the President to punish political enemies for his own political gain. He was forced to deliver tapes that recorded conversations he had in the White House that ultimately showed his involvement in the Watergate break-in.

Gene Basset, 1974, courtesy of United Features Syndicate

James MacGregor Burns observed of Nixon, "How can one evaluate such an idiosyncratic president, so brilliant and so morally lacking?"[76]

Nixon's biographers disagree on how he will be perceived by history. According to Ambrose, "Nixon wanted to be judged by what he accomplished. What he will be remembered for is the nightmare he put the country through in his second term and for his resignation."[77]

Historian Keith W. Olson has written that Nixon left a negative legacy: fundamental mistrust of government, with roots in Vietnam and Watergate.[78]

---

[76] Max J. Skidmore (2001), "Ranking and Evaluating Presidents: The Case of Theodore Roosevelt," *White House Studies* 1 (4), p. 495

[77] Stephen E. Ambrose (1991). *Nixon: Ruin and Recovery 1973–1990.* New York: Simon & Schuster, p. 492, ISBN: 978-0-671-69188-2

[78] Herbert S. Parmet, Richard *Nixon and His America,* Little, Brown & Co.: Boston, 1990, ISBN: 978-0-316-69232-8, p. 81

George Washington summed it up:

"In times of turbulence, when passions are afloat, calm reason is swallowed up in the extremes to which measures are attempted to be carried; but when those subside and the empire of it is resumed, the man who acts from principle, who pursues the paths of truth, moderation, and justice, will regain his influence."[79]

President William Jefferson Clinton, State of the Union
Address, 1997, courtesy of Library of Congress

Character is a journey, not a destination.

— William J. Clinton

The Impeachment of Bill Clinton

Bill Clinton was one of the most popular presidents in U.S. history. He had a strong record of achievement and was judged on his accomplishments.

---

79 From a letter from Washington to John Jay, May 18, 1786, quoted in *The Life of John Marshall,* Albert J. Beveridge, Boston: Houghton Mifflin, 1919, vol. I, p. 307 (http://www.leaderu.com/humanities/foundersview.html)

Tom Toles 1994 cartoon; Clinton was
all things to all people, courtesy of Conservapedia

He was elected twice and managed to maintain a sound economy and a distinctive foreign policy. Even so, he was plagued by questions about his character before and during his time in the White House.

Several women came forward during the election campaign, accusing him of affairs.

There were also allegations of misuse of campaign funds and improprieties when he was Governor of Arkansas.

In the White House, he demonstrated that he was one of the most successful political fund raisers in presidential history, but another scandal developed from this. He was accused of making the Lincoln Bedroom available for overnight stays to contributors. The Democratic Party was also forced to return donations from foreign sources raised by Clinton.

Readings of the Articles of Impeachment against President Clinton in the Senate, January 1999. This was the second time in U.S. history a President faced impeachment, courtesy of National Archives.

His gravest challenge was when he faced impeachment based on allegations of perjury and obstruction of justice arising from his affair with intern Monica Lewinsky. Clinton was exonerated.[80]

On his last day in office, January 20, 2001, President Clinton issued 141 pardon and 36 commutations, some of which were highly questionable.[81]

Bill Neikirk of the Chicago Tribune commented on Clinton's legacy:[82]

Admired by friend and foe for his political skills, Clinton survived eight bruising years of scandal and partisan clashes with congressional Republicans while presiding over one of the best economies in U.S. history...Clinton brought to Washington a new style of governing, the so-called permanent campaign, in which partisan charge is met with partisan countercharge, and legislative battles are often fought like political races. Sometimes this worked to win passage of legislation, but sometimes it created hard feelings and a lack of compromise.

---

[80] "Clinton's Legacy after 8 Years in Office: Peace, Prosperity, and Impeachment," December 14, 2000, by William Neikirk, *Chicago Tribune*, Washington Bureau (http://articles.chicagotribune .com/2000-12-14/news/0012140240_1_clinton-and-gore-legacy-bill-clinton/2)
[81] "Clinton Pardons: Cast of Characters," BBC News Online, February 22, 2001, September 11, 2011
[82] Ibid. Neikirk

*It's a destructive cycle that has been unleashed in American politics,"
said Rep. Mark Sanford (R-S.C.), "and it appears to be here to stay
in a world of 24-hour news cycles," he said... "Bill Clinton's legacy as
president has been burnished by peace and prosperity, tarnished by
impeachment, and ... diminished by the failure of Vice President Al
Gore to succeed him."*

The Nixon and Clinton examples are clear. Character is essential for a
president of the United States. Past words and actions often predict
what their administration will look like and what measures they will take
in matters of state. The "blackmail factor" is also a serious concern. A
president who plays loose with the truth and morals subjects himself and
the nation to extortion.

This is a risk that should never be taken.

In "The Double-Edged Sword, How Character Makes and Ruins
Presidents, from Washington to Clinton," Robert Shogan explained the
importance of character:[83]

*Yet for all the distortions and confusions surrounding the character
issue during the Clinton presidency, the constant controversy serves
only to underline the reality that presidential character remains a
powerful element in the political system and, given the limitations of
that system, a potentially constructive force. Moreover, given the highly
personalized nature of the U.S. political system, politicians and scholars
alike argue that there is no better way of choosing a candidate for
president than by evaluating what kind of human being he--or she-
-really is. "Voters know that the issues a president will have to face
will change in time," Robert Teeter, a GOP pollster and senior Bush
campaign strategist, once told me. "But his character will always be
there." And these words from a contemporary political operative reflect
thinking that has prevailed in the Republic since its founders met two
centuries ago in Constitution Hall.*

---

[83] *The Double-Edged Sword, How Character Makes and Ruins Presidents, From Washington to Clinton,*
Robert Shogan, Westview Press: New York, 1999, Chapter One (https://www.nytimes.com/books/first/s/
shogan-sword.html)

The qualities of a great man are vision, integrity, courage, understanding, the power of articulation, and profundity of character.

— Dwight D. Eisenhower

Character is a word that seems to define almost all human activity and then some...Power is what you do and character is what you are... All leaders must face some crisis where their own strength of character is the enemy. **— Richard Reeves**

What's in a person's heart and soul will not likely be changed by the ability to command a helicopter to land on the South Lawn.

— Robert Dallek

The (ancient) Greeks believed that character was formed in part by fate and in part by parental training, and that character was exemplified not only by acts of bravery in battle, but in the habits of daily conduct.

— James Cannon

In a president, character is everything. A president does not have to be brilliant... He does not have to be clever; you can hire clever... You can hire pragmatic, and you can buy and bring in policy wonks. But you cannot buy courage and decency; you cannot rent a strong moral sense. A president must bring those things with him... He needs to have, in that much maligned word, but a good one nonetheless, a 'vision' of the future he wishes to create... But a vision is worth little if a president does not have the character-- the courage and heart-- to see it through.

— Peggy Noonan

The challenge in selecting a leader is discovering their character to see if their temperaments are what we need today.

Do we need a "Guardian" who will seek cooperation and will follow rules carefully?

Is an "Idealist," who preaches hope and optimism to reach our goals, what we require?

Would a pragmatic, charismatic "Artisan" who looks for immediate results despite the obstacles, be more appropriate for our time of rapid change?

Or would we be better off with a "Rational" leader, who will get the job done, no matter what?

PART TWO: Leadership Qualities of The Commander in Chief
CHAPTER SIX: ━━━━━━━━━━━━
Visionary

Vision is the art of seeing what is invisible to others.

— J. Swift

Leadership is the capacity to translate vision into reality.

— Warren Bennis

You are not here merely to make a living. You are here to enable the world to live more amply, with greater vision, with a finer spirit of hope and achievement. You are here to enrich the world, and you impoverish yourself if you forget the errand.

— Woodrow Wilson

Failed plans should not be interpreted as a failed vision. Visions do not change; they are only refined. Plans rarely stay the same and are scrapped or adjusted as needed. Be stubborn about the vision, but flexible with your plan.

— John C. Maxwell

Where there is no vision, there is no hope.

— George W. Carver

If art is to nourish the roots of our culture, society must set the artist free to follow his vision wherever it takes him.

— John F. Kennedy

> *Vision without action is a daydream. Action without vision is a nightmare.*
>
> **— Japanese Proverb**
>
> *The only thing worse than being blind is having sight but no vision.*
>
> **— Helen Keller**

Our most effective presidents have matched political courage with a compelling vision, which they transmitted to the nation to harness the people's energy and support, and to persuade the country's political institutions to try to reach new goals. A president must have the wherewithal to carry out his or her vision.

Effective presidents need a team of experts to help them govern and garner congressional support for their policies. They must focus on a few key issues and get them approved and implemented.

Bill Clinton, for instance, stated from the start that one of his objectives was to balance the budget and develop a close relationship with business, while still maintaining social programs. Other presidents projected the same sort of aspirations. An example is the U.S. space program

Apollo XI moon landing, July 20, 1969, courtesy of National Archives

Things do not happen. Things are made to happen.

— **John F. Kennedy**

John F. Kennedy: A Man on the Moon

On May 25, 1961, President John F. Kennedy delivered a special message before Congress. He asked for additional funds to begin a concerted effort to create a new space program. He said:[84]

"I believe that this nation should commit itself to achieving the goal, before this decade is out, of landing a man on the moon and returning him safely to the earth. No single space project in this period will be more impressive to mankind, or more important for the long-range exploration of space."

There were some who questioned the National Aeronautics and Space Administration's (NASA) ability to achieve this vision. Yet, within 12 months, Gus Grissom and Alan Shepard became the first two U.S astronauts to travel into space.

In February 1962, John Glenn orbited the earth. He circled the planet three times in four hours and piloted his spaceship, Friendship 7, back into earth's atmosphere, landing in the Atlantic Ocean. His success inspired more attempts to successfully venture into space.

President John Fitzgerald Kennedy, courtesy of JFK Library

---

[84] "John F. Kennedy's Vision of Peace," on the 50th anniversary of JFK's death, his nephew recalls the fallen president's attempts to halt the war machine; by Robert F. Kennedy Jr., November 20, 2013 (http://www.rollingstone.com/politics/news/john-f-kennedys-vision-of-peace-20131120)

Eight years after Kennedy launched his vision for a lunar landing, Apollo 11 astronauts Armstrong, Collins, and Aldrin landed on the moon on July 20, 1969, realizing JFK's dream.

A man may die, nations may rise and fall, but an idea lives on.

— John F. Kennedy

President Ronald Reagan, courtesy of Ronald Reagan Presidential Library

I call upon the scientific community in our country, those who gave us nuclear weapons, to turn their great talents now to the cause of mankind and world peace: to give us the means of rendering these nuclear weapons impotent and obsolete.

— Ronald Reagan

Ronald Reagan's Vision for America

Ronald Reagan had a vision for America. He expressed it on November 3, 1980. It was the night before the election.[85] He began his address by speaking about his faith in our nation's values, and our sense of patriotism and our achievements. He knew that some had doubts about America's future. He wanted to sweep away any concerns. Reagan asked a question and then provided the answer: "The question before us tonight... Does history still have a place for America, for her people, for her great ideals?"[86]

Ronald Reagan laid out the principles of freedom and democracy and justice that he felt were at the heart of the American Dream.

He explained how the dream was still there and would be realized by a government that reduced excessive spending, diminished taxes, fortified its military, worked closely with Congress, and sought peace with all nations through strength and understanding. Reagan ended his address to the voters by emphasizing our common beliefs in our nation's future.

He saw America as the "last best hope of man on earth."

He spoke of those Americans visiting Washington and looking at those symbols of greatness, from the White House to Congress to the Lincoln Memorial, as they repeated Lincoln's words: "Let us bind up the nation's wounds."

He ended his speech this way: [87]

> At this very moment, some young American, coming up along the Virginia or Maryland shores of the Potomac, is seeing for the first time the lights that glow on the great halls of our government and the monuments to the memory of our great men.

---

[85] Ronald Reagan: "Election Eve Address: 'A Vision for America,'" November 3, 1980, online by Gerhard Peters and John T. Woolley, The American Presidency Project (http://www.presidency.ucsb.edu/ws/?pid=85199)
[86] Ibid. Peters and Woolley
[87] Ibid. Peters and Woolley

Let us resolve tonight that young Americans will always see those Potomac lights; that they will always find there a city of hope in a country that is free. And let us resolve that they will say of our day and our generation that we did keep faith with our God, that we did act "worthy of ourselves," that we did protect and pass on lovingly that shining city on a hill.

Reagan won the election with 489 electoral votes against 49 for Carter, carrying 44 states and receiving over 50% of the popular vote against Carter's 41%. Reagan's party captured the Senate and gained seats in the House, where the Democrats retained control.

IT'S MOURNING in AMERICA
Ronald Reagan
1911~2004

Cartoon by Steve Benson, 2004, courtesy of Political Memes

Reagan labored to fulfill his promises. He worked with an opposition Congress to pass legislation to lower taxes and stimulate economic growth, curb inflation, deregulate economic activity, and shrink government spending while expanding military expenditures.

During his eight years in office, inflation fell from 12.5% to 3.4%, and average annual real GDP growth was over 3.4%.[88] He won re-election with the largest Electoral College victory in history. When he left office in 1989, Ronald Reagan departed with an approval rating of 68%, comparable to that of FDR and Bill Clinton.

---

[88] Robert K. Murray, Tim H. Blessing, *Greatness in the White House*, Penn State Press: 1993, p. 80

Freedom is never more than one generation away from extinction. We did not pass it to our children in the bloodstream. It must be fought for, protected, and handed on for them to do the same.

— **Ronald Reagan**

President Theodore Roosevelt, courtesy of the White House

Great thoughts speak only to the thoughtful mind, but great actions speak to all mankind.... Believe you can and you're halfway there.

Far better is it to dare mighty things, to win glorious triumphs, even though checkered by failure ... than to rank with those poor spirits who neither enjoy nor suffer much, because they live in a gray twilight that knows not victory nor defeat.

We must treat each man on his worth and merits as a man. We must see that each is given a square deal, because he is entitled to no more and should receive no less.

— **Theodore Roosevelt**

Theodore Roosevelt and the Square Deal

The 26th President of the United States came into office after the assassination of William McKinley.

He was the youngest man ever to occupy the office.

At first, he pledged to continue his predecessor's policies. Soon he discovered that he had a different vision for America.

Theodore Roosevelt was a man of energy and adventure. He was audacious and exuberant and saw the nation he governed through the same eyes. Roosevelt possessed amazing mental and physical vigor. He was a man of action. He did not hesitate to decide, plot a course, and follow it until it was concluded.

The presidency for Theodore Roosevelt was a "Bully Pulpit."

From that vantage point, he could shape and direct the course of the nation with his ideas, his ideals, and his immense capacity to move forward in all directions simultaneously. He was at the same time a writer, a student, a negotiator, a doer, and a thinker. He believed that the president should set the example in all things and guide the republic to new heights of opportunity and social justice.

Roosevelt cast his vision for America in his "Square Deal."

As the century turned from the 19th to the 20th, he could see the direction of the United States as the juggernaut of the industrial revolution raced forward, engulfing workers, the environment, resources, and institutions.

He saw his mission as controlling savage capitalism, protecting the rights of workers, safeguarding the health and welfare of all Americans, and securing the rights granted in the Constitution to the weak and downtrodden.

The spirit of the Square Deal was about the future.

It was about opening new possibilities and not being afraid of the unknown.

Harper's Weekly, 1904

According to the website "Almanac of Theodore Roosevelt," he was the first president to own an automobile and ride in an airplane. He dove in a submarine, installed a phone in his home, and was the first to travel outside the U.S. while in office, and the first president to receive the first electoral vote cast by a woman delegate. He advocated a Jewish homeland in Palestine, fought for the creation of the League of Nations, and was the first U.S. president to play host to the Olympics. He broke ground on the largest public works project in American history, the Panama Canal. He wrote thirty books and 150,000 letters.

Theodore Roosevelt was the first American citizen to win the Nobel Price and the first and only president to win the Congressional Medal of Honor.

The highest award given by the NCAA bears the name of Theodore Roosevelt. He is featured on the bonds of the United States. His picture is on the $1 Million US Treasury Bill and T Bond.[89]

---

[89] (http://www.theodore-roosevelt.com/trbioqf.html, The Almanac of Theodore Roosevelt website)

Roosevelt won the election of 1904 by a landslide and continued his vision for America by securing the place of the U.S. in the world as a great power. He launched the "Great White Fleet," negotiated the peace treaty ending the Russo-Japanese War, and led a foreign policy of peace with respect and strength. He left the White House in 1908 as one of the most popular leaders in American history.

Mount Rushmore: Washington, Jefferson, Theodore Roosevelt, and Lincoln, courtesy of Library of Congress

Theodore Roosevelt was an American nationalist who projected a view of America as an exceptional country that could succeed in all it ventured. His strategy focused on the president as a visionary and active participant in the life of the nation. His legacy of courage and tenacity of the American spirit has carried on to the present day.

> *Vision and strategy are both important. But there is a priority to them. Vision always comes first. Always. If you have a clear vision, you will eventually attract the right strategy. If you do not have a clear vision, no strategy will save you.*

— Michael Hyatt

The domestic and foreign policy trials that America and democracies will face for the rest of the 21st century demand direction.

The Commander in Chief must visualize and express where we must go and how we will get there in international and domestic affairs, social and economic policy, and the preservation of freedom that needs to be assured to our republic and freedom-loving people.

PART TWO: Leadership Qualities of The Commander in Chief
CHAPTER SEVEN:
Emotional Intelligence

If your emotional abilities aren't in hand, if you don't have self-awareness, if you are not able to manage your distressing emotions, if you can't have empathy and have effective relationships, then no matter how smart you are, you are not going to get very far.

— Daniel Goleman

What makes a leader? . . . self-awareness, which both lets you know your strengths and limits, and strengthens your inner ethical radar; self-management, which lets you lead yourself effectively; and empathy, which lets you read other people accurately. You put all those together in every act of leadership.

— Daniel Goleman

As human beings we all want to be happy and free from misery... we have learned that the key to happiness is inner peace. The greatest obstacles to inner peace are disturbing emotions such as anger, attachment, fear, and suspicion, while love and compassion and a sense of universal responsibility are the sources of peace and happiness.

— Dalai Lama

Sooner or later, those who win are those who think they can.

— Richard Bach

> *Harmonious Emotional Engagement is the tool that allows leaders to take full advantage of these three simple but profound principles: People respond emotionally to every situation that occurs in an organization. People's negative emotions reduce their performance in an organization. People's positive emotions enhance their performance in an organization.*

> **— Timothy Warneka**

> *We often hear that men are unfit to govern themselves. Are they then fit to govern others?*

> **— Thomas Jefferson**

The Components of Emotional Intelligence

A president who wishes to lead others must first be able to lead themselves. Knowing and managing ourselves is the key.

Emotional intelligence is at the epitome of Presidential Leadership. It allows us to tap into our emotions and those of others. Daniel Goleman defined emotional intelligence as consisting of five components: [90]

Self-Awareness

Understanding and recognizing personal emotions, moods, and drives, and their impact on others. This includes honest self-assessment, a self-deprecating sense of humor, and self-confidence.

Self-Regulation

Suspending judgment and thinking before acting, and the ability to redirect and control moods, feelings, and impulses.

Characteristics include integrity, comfort with ambiguity, and change and trustworthiness.

---

[90] Salon, June 28, 1999, Daniel Goleman, "The Five Components of Emotional Intelligence" (http://www.sonoma.edu/users/s/swijtink/teaching/philosophy_101/paper1/goleman.htm)

Internal Motivation

An inner drive that does not involve external rewards. It consists of a passion for work that does not involve status and money, but entails an inner vision of life's priorities, like the love of learning, curiosity, the joy of achievement and activity, pursuit of goals, and persistence and energy. Traits are optimism, a powerful drive to accomplish, even in the face of failure, and loyalty to an institution and its objectives.

Empathy

Comprehending the emotional temperament of others and treating people based on their emotional responses. Qualities are retaining talent, cross-cultural understanding, sincere sympathy, service to others, and altruism.

Social Skills

Ability to build and manage relationships, find common ground for understanding and creating support. Traits are success in handling change, the ability to persuade, and skill in constructing and leading teams.

When it comes to having emotional intelligence, we must match it with normal, rational behavior and overall health.

The White House is no place for those who are emotionally disturbed or have severe mental illnesses or are not physically fit to handle the enormous responsibilities of President of the United States. Those who have emotional intelligence also have the wisdom to know how to maintain equilibrium by relaxing and resting sufficiently.

Lincoln went to the theater, John Kennedy and Franklin Roosevelt loved sailing. In each case, they were able to focus on relieving the great burden of responsibility, to preserve their mental and physical strength to carry out their duties.

Several presidents exhibited the form of strong emotional intelligence explained by Goleman. They include Lincoln, Jefferson, Washington, Kennedy, Franklin Roosevelt, and Theodore Roosevelt.[91]

Abraham Lincoln, courtesy Library of Congress

Nearly all men can stand adversity, but if you want to test a man's character, give him power.

— Abraham Lincoln

---

[91] Bruce R. Posten, "The power of EQ: Emotional intelligence can make big difference in a president's success" (http://www2.readingeagle.com/article.aspx?id=125717)

Lincoln's Strength, Empathy, Compassion and Moral Compass

Lincoln had high morals, kindness, steadfastness, vision, sterling character, and wisdom. His leadership was challenged constantly. He certainly had powerful emotional intelligence to deal with the endless obstacles and difficulties that would have overcome most leaders. For example, he suffered from: the loss of his young sons; the division of the Union; defeats on the battlefield; the enormous causalities of the war; the criticism of the press, his staff, and his cabinet; and the capricious behavior of his wife.

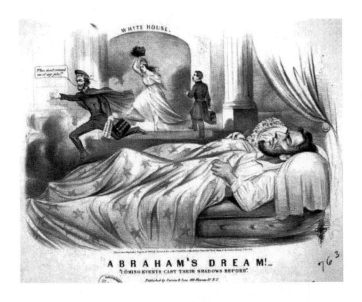

Abraham's dream! – "Coming events cast their shadows before," 1864, Currier and Ives

He handled constant setbacks by staying focused on his goals: win the war, preserve the Union, end slavery, and Reconstruction.

He set aside egos, ambitions, and conflicts in his Cabinet and personal attacks on him by staying the course of his vision, which he constantly articulated and explained. Lincoln rarely insisted that he was right when others contested his opinions and decisions. He listened and was ready to change his mind if need be.

Often, Lincoln would write a letter channeling his emotions and venting his anger when he was opposed or criticized. He would save it for a day or two and rarely send it. It gave him time to cool down and use reason and common sense and not make rash judgements that would result in more conflict.

One of his greatest talents was his ability to listen patiently to both sides of an argument. Those who had the opportunity to discuss issues with him felt that Lincoln gave them the chance to express themselves, even if he disagreed.

He spoke in simple, clear language that his audience could understand and learn from. He never spoke above his audience. He used stories and metaphors to transform complex ideas into simple concepts that all could grasp.

Lincoln was a skillful mediator. He brought those of differing opinions together to discuss and resolve issues. He showed a remarkable ability to consider the feelings of others. He made it a point to mend fences with his enemies and not humiliate them in the process.

He had the courage to be kind.

Perhaps his greatest emotional strength was his humility. He was self-confident enough to admit and learn from his errors and flexible enough to change course.

He always took responsibility.

He admitted his mistakes and did not dwell on them or those of others. He preferred to move on and get the job done.

Lincoln never denigrated his enemies with vile or foul language or resorted to personal attacks on them or their families and followers. He focused on policies, ideas, and ideals, and maintained the high ground as a gentleman, a leader, and a human being.

As the Civil War concluded, Abraham Lincoln did not gloat over his victory. He went to great lengths to avoid humiliating the South and its leaders. General Robert E. Lee, for example, was treated with dignity. Confederate soldiers could go home with their possessions.

On February 15, 1865, two months before the end of the Civil War and his assassination, *The New York Times* wrote about Lincoln and his emotional intelligence and his place in history:[92]

In fact, when we take into account the circumstances in which Mr. LINCOLN has been placed, the provocations he has received, the excitement in the midst of which he has lived, and the vile and blackguard personal abuse which has during the last four years been showered on him, both here and in Europe, it will always reflect the highest honor on him, as well as on the people whom he represents, that he has never once been betrayed into violent or even impatient language. We believe his speeches and letters may be searched in vain for the smallest indication of passion or vexation.

There are many things in them which a scholar or man of high culture would, perhaps, have omitted, or have uttered differently, but nothing which a gentleman might regret or feel ashamed of. This consolation, and it is a great one, he will at least carry with him into his retirement...

Thomas Jefferson, courtesy of Library of Congress

---

[92] *The New York Times*, February 15, 1865, "Jefferson Davis and Lincoln" (http://www.nytimes.com/1865/02/15/news/jefferson-davis-abraham-lincoln.html)

Nothing can stop the man with the right mental attitude from achieving his goal; nothing on earth can help the man with the wrong mental attitude.

Do you want to know who you are? Do not ask. Act! Action will delineate and define you.

Honesty is the first chapter in the book of wisdom.

—Thomas Jefferson

Thomas Jefferson: A Model of Presidential Leadership

"When a group of Nobel laureates visited the White House during his administration, John F. Kennedy remarked, 'I think this is the most extraordinary collection of talent, of human knowledge, that has ever been gathered together at the White House, with the possible exception of when Thomas Jefferson dined alone.'"[93]

Jefferson was a founding father, and the principal author of the Declaration of the Independence. He reflected strong emotional intelligence throughout his life and certainly during his presidency. He was multitalented and multifaceted. In each of Jefferson's activities, he had to exhibit self-control and self-restraint. He was a model of presidential leadership.

Abraham Lincoln articulated Jefferson's principles of liberty and freedom as the reasons to preserve the Union. He called him, "the most distinguished politician in our history."[94] He was a Renaissance man who was skilled in so many areas in addition to politics. One of Jefferson's biographers called him a man who "could calculate an eclipse, survey an estate, tie an artery, plan an edifice, try a cause, break a horse, dance a minuet, and play the violin."[95]

---

[93]John F. Kennedy, "Remarks at a Dinner Honoring Nobel Prize Winners of the Western Hemisphere," April 29, 1962 (http://www.presidency.ucsb.edu/ws/?pid=8623)
[94] Ibid. John F. Kennedy
[95] Ibid. John F. Kennedy

Professor James Barber wrote about Jefferson's achievements as president and cited him as one of the most accomplished leaders in our history, because he "was able to apply his reason to organizing connections with Congress and was thus able to express a clear and open vision of what the country could be with a profound political sense."[96] Jefferson was able to interact with all types of people at all levels. He dealt with policy advocates in Congress, with politicians and ordinary people. He had a clear sense of vision and was able to portray it with common sense and pragmatism.

"In a paper on presidential leadership, Sarah Ofosu-Ameyaw, describes how, 'Jefferson's ability to apply reason and clearly express his vision of what this country should be, shows that he is indeed an individual who had a high level of emotional intelligence; he was emotionally self-aware, assertive, he had a high self-regard, he was capable of problem solving, and he had good impulse control.'"[97] This was the key to his success. He was able to empathize and sympathize, manage his emotions, and comprehend those of others.

Few American presidents are held in higher esteem than Thomas Jefferson... he holds an unshakable place in the pantheon of American heroes.

— Robert Dallek

Jefferson had almost single-handedly provided 'a mine of legislative wealth' that provided Virginians with a modern republic built on the foundations of Greece and Rome... Jefferson, in short, in his legal laboratory atop Monticello, invented the United States of America.

— Willard Sterne Randall

---

[96] Russel Razzague, MD, "Top 3 Emotionally Intelligent Presidents in US History, Part 1: Thomas Jefferson" (https://www.psychologytoday.com/blog/political-intelligence/201203/top-3-emotionally-intelligent-presidents-in-us-history-part-1)
[97] Ibid. Razzague

Other presidents also exhibited the kind of emotional intelligence that helped guide America during its most difficult times.

George Washington, courtesy of Library of Congress

The Self-Confidence of George Washington

His strength of character commanded the kind of respect and awe necessary for our first president. Washington proved on the battlefield and in the field of politics that he had self-control, self-respect, and respect and admiration for others. His self-confidence allowed him to deal with the strong personalities of his Cabinet and face the challenges of the young republic he led. He understood the use of power and set the foundation for the Presidency to be occupied by those who were patriotic, experienced, honorable, and committed to sacrificing all they had for the United States.

Franklin Delano Roosevelt, courtesy of Library of Congress

The Resilience of FDR

Justice Oliver Wendell Holmes said: "FDR had a second-class intellect, but a first class temperament."[98] His charm, wit, charisma, ability to communicate, and his skill at self-control gave him the strength to deal with the tremendous challenges of the Great Depression and World War II.

Our nation was fortunate that he was at the helm during those critical times and surrounded himself with advisers who also had emotional intelligence to tackle the critical problems of his era.

Ronald Reagan, courtesy of Reagan Presidential Library

The Optimism of Ronald Reagan

He projected a simple, friendly, optimistic personality. He conveyed trustworthiness and rarely took himself seriously. Like Lincoln, he used humor to make a point and drive home an idea. Mikhail Gorbachev described Reagan this way: "While adhering to his convictions, Reagan was not dogmatic; he was looking for negotiation and compromise." Those who worked with him found him kind, humble, and a decent person who was devoid of pettiness and meanness. He admitted mistakes and moved on. Ronald Reagan sought a balanced and full life while leading the nation. He had the emotional intelligence to do both.[99]

---

[98] Ibid. Posten
[99] Ibid. Posten

Dr. Heather Uczynski has studied the emotional intelligence of several presidents. Her observations are interesting in that they clearly demonstrate that without it a president cannot handle the awesome burden of responsibilities that go with the job.[100]

Dwight David Eisenhower, courtesy of Library of Congress

IKE's Ability to Persuade without Dominating

According to Uczynski, Eisenhower had the ability to be persuasive without being domineering. He had a way of saying the right things to elicit cooperation and trust. As Supreme Allied Commander in World War II, he had to contend with numerous personalities and political leaders to harness the energy of the Allies to win the war.

He was a natural leader with a strong character, matched by a good nature. His experience as a military leader and administrator gave him the skills to organize the White House and set up a team to deal with the growing challenges of the Cold War.

---

[100] Ibid. Posten

Theodore Roosevelt, courtesy of Library of Congress

Theodore Roosevelt: Powerful Emotional Intelligence

Uczynski judged Teddy Roosevelt as one "perfectly fitted for his times."
He had powerful emotional intelligence, which he exhibited by his energy,
decisiveness, and assertiveness. He was self-aware but seemed, at times,
to lack self-control.[101]

Teddy was a volcano of energy.

He maintained a vigorous schedule of meetings, speeches, physical and
mental activity, and constantly making decisions. He exhibited fearlessness
and a profound vision of where America should be going, and how to get
there. Roosevelt consistently articulated his vision of a strong, free, and
prosperous country that was creative and compassionate.

He matched his rhetoric with actions, like flying in the first plane to promote
the new technology, and passing legislation to build the Panama Canal to
unite the East and West Coasts into a well-organized system of trade on the
high seas, which would expand global commerce and make America more
secure militarily and economically.

---

[101] Ibid. Posten

Courtesy of the Truman Library

Truman: Unafraid to Decide

Harry Truman had extraordinarily strong emotional intelligence and was not afraid to make decisions and move forward, even if they were not of political benefit to him or his party.

He was disciplined, with integrity and self-confidence and respect for the Office of President.

After the death of Franklin Roosevelt, Harry Truman was left with the tasks of ending the Wars in Europe and Japan and securing a post-war peace. He did so by making tough but well thought out decisions. They required the discipline and rigor to choose alternatives based on facts, and sticking to them. This demanded steadfastness on his part and those of his team.

Nicholas Garland, courtesy of *The New Statesman*, November 25, 1977

Jimmy Carter and Camp David

Jimmy Carter showed during the Camp David Accords his firmness, as well as his sense of caring for the welfare of both sides. He brought Egypt's President Sadat and Israel Prime Minister Begin to come to an agreement that seemed impossible to achieve. During the Iranian hostage crisis, he stayed focused, poised, and calm. Yet he was accused of not being close to the Washington establishments, with a tendency to micromanage.

Dr. Ucynski believed several presidents had low emotional intelligence.

Richard Nixon, in her view, was paranoid and kept grudges. He did not have an easy good humor or the social skills of most politicians. He was demanding and often disregarded the feelings of others, in her opinion.

Lyndon Johnson was energetic, but compulsive and manipulative, and could be deceptive and cunning to a fault. Johnson, like Nixon, often viewed criticism as personal attacks.

Clinton was brilliant, but lacked self-discipline. Hoover, Coolidge, and Wilson, she relates, were different types of leaders, but shared an introverted nature. This worked against their effectiveness. Instead of appearing outgoing and friendly, they were austere and cold and "sometimes easily irritated and overwhelmed by stress."[102]

---

[102] Ibid. Posten (http://www2.readingeagle.com/article.aspx?id=125717)

Franklin Roosevelt's Fatal Secret

Last known photo of Franklin Roosevelt, on the afternoon
of April 11, 1945; he died the next day. Courtesy of National Archives

In 2011, newspaper reports came out concerning a seven-decade
old letter about the health of Franklin Delano Roosevelt while he was
campaigning for the presidency for an unprecedented fourth time.

On July 10, 1944, Dr. Frank Lahey, Chairman of the Directing Board for
Physicians, Dentists, and Veterinarians of the War Manpower Commission
of the Office of Emergency Management, wrote a confidential memo
citing his objections and concerns about the health of the president.

Dr. Frank Lahey, courtesy of National Archives

Lahey was a prominent doctor and surgeon. He had personally examined the president and recorded his findings and discussed them with FDR, directly.

He recommended that he not seek a fourth term and that if he did, to find an appropriate Vice President to succeed him. This information was also given to Democratic Party leaders who would select the candidate for the 1944 presidential election.

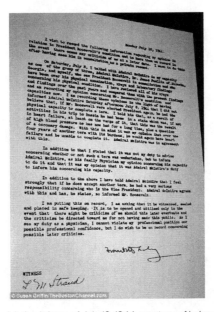

Dr. Frank Lahey's letter of July 10, 1944, courtesy of Lahey Clinic

The president's health had been declining for years. The stress of the job laid heavily on his shoulders. It had affected his entire being and was now snuffing out his life.

Franklin Roosevelt knew he was going to die.

He knew he would not finish his last term in office. As a result, he changed Vice Presidents and chose a little know senator from Missouri named Harry S. Truman, who party leaders believed was capable of succeeding FDR.[103]

---

[103] Daniel Bates, Mail Online, April 11, 2011, memo that warned Franklin D. Roosevelt he would die if he ran for a fourth term

Dr. Lahey had examined the president. He felt it was necessary to go on record and explain his diagnosis if someone, someday, would question it.

The president was informed in July 1944 that he was going to die, according to Dr. Lahey's letter.

The doctor predicted that Roosevelt would be gone within a year.

He died ten months later, from a massive stroke.

Steven Lomazow, co-author of *FDR's Deadly Secret*, stated: "It is quite evident that FDR was well aware of his diagnosis and prognosis prior to accepting the Democratic nomination for the presidency."

Questions circulated during the start of the fourth term as to FDR's physical and mental health, and his ability to continue as president. Franklin Roosevelt's travelling Secretary, William D. Hassett, recorded this in his diary of March 30, 1945:[104]

"FDR returned from the 14,000-mile trip to the Yalta Conference on February 28, 1945. The next day, he appeared before a Joint Session of Congress to report on the conference. His delivery of the speech was erratic, and he made frequent rambling departures from the written text. The President remained in Washington until March 24, when he went home to Hyde Park for a few days. He returned to Washington on March 29 for a day, and then continued to Warm Springs. Everyone hoped that Warm Springs would rejuvenate the President, as it had always done before."

The president was naturally exhausted from the voyage. He mentioned it in his remarks to the Congress: "I hope that you will pardon me for this unusual posture of sitting down during the presentation of what I want to say, but I know that you will realize that it makes it a lot easier for me not to have to carry about ten pounds of steel around on the bottom of my legs; and also because of the fact that I have just completed a fourteen-thousand-mile trip."[105]

---

[104] "FDR's Health, Diary of Presidential Secretary William D. Hassett," March 30, 1945 (http://www.fdrlibraryvirtualtour.org/graphics/07-38/7.5_FDRs_Health.pdf)
[105] The Miller Center of the University of Virginia, "Address to Congress on Yalta," March 1, 1945 (http://millercenter.org/president/fdroosevelt/speeches/speech-3338)

Rumors spread about his inability to act coherently at the Yalta Conference. These raised concerns from those nearest the President. Hassett later recorded in his diary: "He is slipping away and no earthly power can keep him here...To all the staff, to the family and with the Boss himself, I have maintained the bluff; but I am convinced that there is no help for him."

Franklin Roosevelt died in Warm Springs, Georgia, thirteen days later.

In releasing the letter of Dr. Lahey, Dr. John Libertino, director of the Lahey Clinic's Sophia Gordon Cancer Center, stated:

"The real issue is: There is a delicate balance between patient confidentiality and national security. Both issues were in play at the time, so some may view this as a conspiracy, as have some authors. But when you consider the circumstances of the country at the time, it was probably either a political or heroic act by FDR."[106]

Thus, the key question to be faced is should a president be allowed to continue in office if his health is failing?

Woodrow Wilson was incapacitated with a stroke in the last year of his administration. John Kennedy had severe health problems. The public has a right to know not only if the president is physically and mentally capable to continue the job, but also if a candidate for president is fit to take on the awesome burden of President of the United States, physically and mentally.

The head of a nation must have nerves of steel.

There will be moments in the future that test leaders' will and pride.

Who will have the strength, courage, and wisdom to deal with another attack on America and freedom, like 9-11? Who can we trust to protect us and the world from nuclear war? Who will make decisions based on facts, and not on emotions unduly influenced by serious ill health?

---

[106]Carey Goldberg, "Long-Lost 'Lahey Memo' On FDR's Health Unveiled," Common Health, April 8, 2 (http://commonhealth.wbur.org/2011/04/what-killed-fdr)

PART TWO: Leadership Qualities of The Commander in Chief
CHAPTER EIGHT: ▬▬▬▬
Courage and Wisdom

It is not the critic who counts; not the man who points out how the strong man stumbles, or where the doer of deeds could have done them better. The credit belongs to the man who is actually in the arena, whose face is marred by dust and sweat and blood, who strives valiantly, who errs and comes up short again and again ... who spends himself in a worthy cause; who at the best knows, in the end, the triumph of high achievement, and who at the worst, if he fails, at least he fails while daring greatly.

— T. Roosevelt

You gain strength, courage, and confidence by every experience in which you really stop to look fear in the face. You are able to say to yourself, "I lived through this horror. I can take the next thing that comes along."

— Eleanor Roosevelt

I learned that courage was not the absence of fear, but the triumph over it. The brave man is not he who does not feel afraid, but he who conquers that fear.

— Nelson Mandela

God grant me the serenity to accept the things I cannot change, the courage to change the things I can, and the wisdom to know the difference.

— Reinhold Niebuhr

In whatever arena of life one may meet the challenge of courage, whatever may be the sacrifices he faces if he follows his conscience – the loss of his friends, his fortune, his contentment, even the esteem of his fellow men – each man must decide for himself the course he will follow.

— **John F. Kennedy**

A president must bring courage and wisdom to the office. It cannot be acquired later. It is part of their character and temperament. It is the reason why he or she is there.

Courage requires sacrifice and risk.

Political courage means taking a stand based on principle, no matter what the consequences. It demands doing the right thing for the people of the United States and the world, even if, at that moment, it appears to be the wrong decision at the wrong time. Such was the case when Gerald Ford pardoned Richard Nixon.

Gerald Ford is sworn in as the 38th President of the United States by Chief Justice Warren Burger in the White House East Room on August 9, 1974. Courtesy of National Archives

Gerald Ford and the Nixon Pardon

On September 8, 1974, President Gerald Ford pardoned his predecessor, Richard Nixon. It was one of the most controversial presidential actions in our history.

Nixon was on the verge of being indicted for the cover-up dealing with the Watergate scandal. He resigned. Less than a month after he took the oath of office, Ford pardoned his predecessor "for all offenses against the United States which he, Richard Nixon, has committed or may have committed or taken part in during the period from January 20, 1969, through August 9, 1974."[107]

Ford knew that history would judge him for pardoning Nixon. He explained to the people why he felt it was necessary.:"It is believed that a trial of Richard Nixon, if it became necessary, could not fairly begin until a year or more has elapsed. In the meantime, the tranquility to which this nation has been restored by the events of recent weeks could be irreparably lost by the prospects of bringing to trial a former President of the United States." Ford was a man of compassion. He added these words to the pardon: "I feel that Richard Nixon and his loved ones have suffered enough."[108]

Ford viewed Watergate as an "American tragedy" that needed to be ended. He knew he was the only one who had the power to end it. With the Nixon pardon, "our long national nightmare" would be concluded, he said. His chief concern was to move ahead with the country's business without the burden of Richard Nixon's trial interfering with the national agenda. Vietnam and the economy were high priority problems that needed the undivided attention of the President of the United States and the Congress.

---

[107] Text of President Ford's Pardon Proclamation, September 08, 1974 (http://watergate.info/1974/09/08/text-of-ford-pardon-proclamation.html)
[108] Caroline Kennedy, *Profiles in Courage for Our Time*, John F. Kennedy Library Foundation: Boston, 2001, p. 295

Ford was almost universally criticized for the pardon. It was a factor that cost him the election of 1976. Forty years after the Nixon pardon, those who were among Ford's harshest critics gathered and looked back at the event. Carl Bernstein and Bob Woodward were the *Washington Post* reporters who uncovered the Watergate scandal. They vehemently criticized Ford at the time. Four decades later, Woodward called the pardon "an act of courage." Bernstein said it took "great courage." Senator Edward Kennedy acknowledged that it was in the best interests of the country. Watergate Prosecutor Richard Ben-Veniste took it even further:

"The decision to pardon Nixon was a political judgment, properly within the bounds of Ford's constitutional authority...Jerry Ford acted in accord with what he sincerely felt were the best interests of the country; that there was no secret quid pro quo with Nixon for a pardon in return for resignation; and that Ford, a compassionate man, was moved by the palpable suffering of a man who had lost so much."[110]

Caroline Kennedy said of him: "Ford's ambition for the country was larger than his own ambition. Restored confidence was more important than his re-election. That's courage."[111]

Franklin Roosevelt with Ruthie Bie and Fala at Hilltop Cottage
in Hyde Park, 1941, courtesy of Franklin Delano Roosevelt Library

---

[110] "The Nixon Pardon in Retrospect, 40 Years Later," September 8, 2014, The National Constitutional Center (http://blog.constitutioncenter.org/2014/09/the-nixon-pardon-in-retrospect-40-years-later/)
[111] Ibid. Caroline Kennedy, pp. 314-315

Franklin Roosevelt and Polio

In 1921, Franklin Delano Roosevelt was considered one of the bright lights of the Democrat Party and a future presidential contender. He had gone to the best schools. He was an accomplished public speaker. He was handsome, charming, charismatic, and witty. He was former Assistant Secretary of the Navy and Vice-Presidential candidate in 1920. Franklin was the cousin of Teddy Roosevelt, one of the most popular leaders in American history.

Like Teddy, he came from a family of wealth and influence. His was a star truly on the rise.

Then, in the summer of 1921, polio struck.

Infantile paralysis became the greatest personal and political hurdle in his life. His illness made the headlines of *The New York Times*. Many thought that his political career was over. Franklin Roosevelt believed this as well. No one in his condition had been elected to high political office in American history.

Louie Howe with FDR in 1932, courtesy of Library of Congress

Two people had faith in him: Eleanor Roosevelt and Louie Howe. Eleanor knew he had the inner strength to overcome his infirmity. Howe was his top political adviser. He saw greatness in Franklin Roosevelt and believed that he would muster the political courage to return to public life. It took FDR three years. He found some relief in the waters of a resort in Warm Springs, Georgia.

Most of all, he found hope.

It was the hope that he could someday walk again that propelled Franklin Roosevelt forward. It was an inner voice that told him that he could persevere and return to advance his political career despite infantile paralysis. It took enormous courage for Roosevelt to take the first steps to rehabilitate himself in the eyes of his party and the eyes of the public.

FDR used crutches when nominating Al Smith at the 1924 Democratic National Convention, the speech that marked his return to public life, June 26, 1924, courtesy of Franklin Delano Roosevelt Library

The great opportunity came during the presidential convention of 1924. Roosevelt was asked to put in nomination the name of Alfred E. Smith, Governor of New York, for President of the United States. The following passage from *Profiles in Leadership: From Caesar to Modern Times* describes Roosevelt's anxiety and how he overcame his fear with the courage of his wife, Eleanor:[112]

"FDR was frightened. He feared his paralysis would cause him to lose control, fall during the convention and show he did not have the stamina to be a leader. Eleanor helped him meet the challenge. She encouraged him. She relieved his fears. She said later that polio taught Franklin what suffering was about. His illness made him stronger.

"Even though he was paralyzed from the waist down and could not move his legs, steel braces helped hold him erect. He learned to toss his lower body out one leg at a time to give the impression of walking while holding on to the arm of his son. Finally, convinced he could succeed, FDR offered to put the governor's name in nomination at the 1924 Democratic Presidential Convention. Smith was delighted.

"It was late June. New York was sweltering. Over a thousand party members huddled into the hot stands of Madison Square Garden. At the Garden, FDR entered through a back door. He wanted to avoid reporters taking photos of him in a wheelchair. He was carried up the stairs, thrown over the back of a strong aide. Behind a curtain, he took up his crutches. He was perspiring. His family was in the wings, watching and waiting. William J. Vanden Heuvel described what followed:

"On the arm of his son, FDR, with his legs firm in locked braces, holding a cane in his other hand, advanced slowly without crutches to the podium in Madison Square Garden. It was a moment that no one who saw it would ever forget. His palpable courage, his lyrical eloquence, his magnificent voice, brought the delegates to their feet – and at that

---

[112] Emilio Iodice, *Profiles in Leadership: From Caesar to Modern Times*, North American Business Press: Miami, FL, 2013, p. 285

moment Franklin Roosevelt resumed a national political career. Seven years after his polio attack, Roosevelt was elected Governor of New York. As Frank Freidel, one of the important Roosevelt biographers, has written, Roosevelt had perfected so effective an illusion of his strength and well-being that most Americans never realized until after his death that he was, in fact, a paraplegic.

"The crowd, spellbound, heard FDR call Smith, 'The Happy Warrior.' After one hundred and three ballots, John W. Davis, former Congressman from West Virginia, was selected. Smith lost the nomination. Calvin Coolidge won another term in office by a landslide. Despite the election outcome, Franklin and Eleanor Roosevelt had a personal and political triumph. It would carry them to the governor's mansion and to the White House."

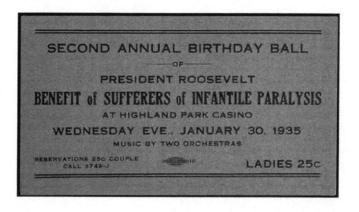

Ticket to a 1935 "Birthday Ball" honoring President Franklin Roosevelt, courtesy of Franklin Delano Roosevelt Library

Eleanor Roosevelt, courtesy of the White House

During his presidency, Franklin Roosevelt worked to raise funds to help the disabled and conduct research for a polio vaccine. Each year, a birthday party would be held in his honor to help the cause. Thanks to him and Eleanor, the March of Dimes was created. On April 12, 1955, the tenth anniversary of the death of FDR, the first results of the successful field test of the Salk vaccine were announced.

Franklin Roosevelt, 1941, courtesy of Franklin Delano Roosevelt Library

Seventeen years after Franklin Roosevelt put the name of Al Smith before the Democrat Convention, he faced another challenge that demanded courage and wisdom.

On January 10, 1941, President Roosevelt introduced Lend-Lease to the U.S. Congress.

The Battle of Britain was raging. The United Kingdom could fall to Nazi Germany at any time. FDR knew that America was the "last bastion of democracy" to help England survive the Nazi onslaught. Lend-Lease permitted military aid to any nation whose security was vital to the United States. It gave the president the power to "lend" military arms to Britain, with the accord that the US would be repaid in kind after the war. Staunch isolationists opposed the plan.

FDR mustered all the political influence and courage at his disposal to get the law passed. It was accepted by the Congress overwhelmingly. The plan gave the United States time to prepare for the rising threat from Japan and Germany. It gave us time to organize our navy and military for a two-front war that would be the greatest challenge America had ever faced.

Little boy receiving a pair of shoes in Europe
after the War, courtesy of George C. Marshall Foundation

Franklin Roosevelt's vision, courage, and political skill, starting with Lend-Lease, laid the foundation for the post-war period and the Marshall Plan to feed the starving millions after WWII and rebuild Europe and Japan.

FDR and the Holocaust

"Progressives have a long and admirable record of honestly acknowledging FDR's failings alongside his achievements. Roosevelt's response to the Holocaust is no more defensible than his internment of Japanese Americans or his troubling record on the rights of African Americans. Recognizing that fact does not endanger the legacy of the New Deal or diminish FDR's accomplishments in bringing America out of the Depression or his leadership in World War II. It merely acknowledges his flaws, as well."

These are the words of Rafael Medoff, Founding Director of the David S. Wyman Institute for Holocaust Studies in a September 2013 article in *The Nation* titled, "FDR and the Holocaust" by Lawrence Zuckerman.

Aerial reconnaissance photograph of Auschwitz concentration camp, showing Auschwitz II (Birkenau) taken by the U.S. Air Force between April 4, 1944, and January 15, 1945 (USHMM Photo Archives).

The Allies knew of the Nazi extermination program at the outset of World War II. In an April 2015 article titled, "Auschwitz Bombing Controversy: Could the Allies Have Bombed Auschwitz-Birkenau?" by Mitchell Bard, in the Jewish Virtual Library, evidence is presented of detailed information about the camps from survivors in 1942. They exhibited data about the mass exterminations and explained how the camps could be bombed and destroyed to stop the killings.

Former Senator George McGovern, a bomber pilot in World War II, stated that his squadron hit Nazi oil facilities less than five miles from Auschwitz. He said in 2005: "There is no question we should have attempted to go after Auschwitz. There was a pretty good chance we could have blasted those rail lines off the face of the earth, which would have interrupted the flow of people to those death chambers, and we had a pretty good chance of knocking out those gas ovens."

At the height of the Holocaust, in 1943, one of FDR's staunchest supporters, journalist Freda Kirchwey, denounced his failure to respond to Nazi genocide.

She wrote, "You and I and the President and the Congress and the State Department are accessories to the crime and share Hitler's guilt," she wrote. "If we had behaved like humane and generous people instead of complacent, cowardly ones, the two million Jews lying today in the earth of Poland and Hitler's other crowded graveyards would be alive and safe.... We had it in our power to rescue this doomed people and we did not lift a hand to do it—or perhaps it would be fairer to say that we lifted just one cautious hand, encased in a tight-fitting glove of quotas and visas and affidavits, and a thick layer of prejudice."

Kirchwey was editor of *The Nation*, a magazine which, as early as 1938, called for the U.S. to rescue Jews after the Kristallnacht when it was clear that millions were in danger. The publication asked for the rescue of 15,000 German-Jewish refugee children.

The Roosevelt Administration refused.

Kirchwey wrote in 1940: "The Roosevelt administration's refugee policy is one which must sicken any person of ordinarily humane instinct. It is as if we were to examine laboriously the curriculum vitae of flood victims clinging to a piece of floating wreckage and finally to decide that no matter what their virtues, all but a few had better be allowed to drown."

Franklin Roosevelt was presented with information about the "Final Solution" by his advisers shortly after the U.S. entered the war. FDR's Secretary of the Treasury and one of his most trusted aides, Henry Morgenthau, said that the U.S. knew of the camps in 1942, according to Michael Beschloss in his 2002 book, *The Conquerors: Roosevelt, Truman, and the Destruction of Hitler's Germany, 1941-1945* (Simon and Shuster). Morgenthau tried to persuade FDR to act, but failed. Secretary of War Henry L. Stimson opposed any assistance measures, as did the Assistant Secretary of War, John J. McCoy, and Secretary of State Cordell Hull.

Beschloss says the Allies failed to deliver "a moral statement for all time that the British and Americans understood the historical gravity of the Holoucast."

Roosevelt refused Morgenthau's repeated exhortations to bomb Auschwitz.

Beschloss argues that FDR remained "shockingly disengaged from the struggle to rescue Jewish refugees from Hitler." He did not try "to explore whether death camp bombings and transportation lines might have saved lives."

Franklin Roosevelt was the most powerful national leader in World War II. He had the power to stop one of the most brutal crimes the world has ever seen. It is an example of the ability of the President of the United States to change the course of history and fight evil, or to allow it to continue its path of destruction and anguish.

Last known photograph of Lincoln taken by Henry F. Warren
on the White House balcony, March 6, 1865, courtesy of Library of Congress

Lincoln and Slavery

By the end of the Civil War, Abraham Lincoln had repeatedly
demonstrated physical, mental, and political courage far beyond any
of our presidents before or after him. He endured constant pressure
from Cabinet members, political opponents, members of his party,
and the press.

He faced assassination threats.

He battled with military officials over the course of the war. He
constantly changed generals and officers until he found General Grant.
He showed bravery in issuing the Emancipation Proclamation. His
closest advisers were against it. They warned him that he would lose
re-election if he issued the Proclamation. Radical Republicans and War
Democrats opposed him. He stuck to his convictions[113]

---

[113] Michael Beschloss, *Presidential Courage: Brave Leaders and How They Changed America, 1789-1989*, Michael
Beschloss, Simon & Schuster: May 2007, as quoted in the book review online on America's Trust (http://ameri-
castrust.us/presidentialcourage.html)

The Emancipation Proclamation was signed on January 1, 1863. It did not immediately end slavery, but it laid the groundwork for passage of the 13th Amendment to the Constitution, which permanently ended slavery in America.

Currier and Ives, 1865

One of Lincoln's last acts of political courage was his Second Inaugural Address on March 4, 1865.

The Civil War was ending. He could have cited his amazing achievements in bringing the nation to victory, eliminating slavery, and preserving the Union. He did not. Instead, Abraham Lincoln removed himself from any accomplishments and offered questions as to why the conflict had happened to begin with. He searched into the conscience of America to reflect on what had happened and what would now confront the nation.

He realized that many who were listening wanted revenge against the South. The people of the North blamed the South for starting the War. They blamed them for the bloodshed and suffering. Many wanted retribution.

Abraham Lincoln wanted forgiveness.

He asked for charity, compassion, and "care for him who shall have borne the battle, and for his widow, and his orphan." Lincoln avoided seeking political correctness in lauding the victories of the North.

He was asking for mercy for the vanquished, "With Malice toward none, with charity for all, with firmness in the right, as God gives us to see the right, let us strive on to finish the work we are in, to bind up the nation's wounds."

It was a magnificent display of courage and wisdom.[114]

Ford's Theatre, the night of Friday, April 14, 1865, courtesy of National Archives

---

[114] Ted Widmer, "And the End Came," *The New York Times*, March 3, 2015

His final act came a month and eleven days later when a member of the audience who listened to him on that chilly March day, John Wilkes Booth, shot him on April 14, 1865, while watching a play in Ford's Theatre in Washington, DC.

Abraham Lincoln died the next day.

Lincoln's example was the courage to do the right thing, despite the personal consequences, even if it might not be the right time.

Situations will arise during the term of an occupant of the White House or a Prime Minister that will test his or her bravery, compassion, and good judgment.

History, despite its wrenching pain, cannot be unlived, but if faced with courage, need not be lived again.

— Maya Angelou

Whatever you do, you need courage. Whatever course you decide upon, there is always someone to tell you that you are wrong. There are always difficulties arising that tempt you to believe your critics are right. To map out a course of action and follow it to an end requires some of the same courage that a soldier needs. Peace has its victories, but it takes brave men and women to win them.

— Ralph Waldo Emerson

Whatever we learn to do, we learn by doing it; men come to be builders, for instance, by building, and harp players by playing the harp. In the same way, by doing just acts we come to be just; by doing self-controlled acts, we come to be self-controlled; and by doing brave acts, we become brave.

— Aristotle

PART TWO: Leadership Qualities of The Commander in Chief
CHAPTER NINE:
Decision Maker

> *Never cut a tree down in the wintertime. Never make a negative decision in the low time. Never make your most important decisions when you are in your worst moods. Wait. Be patient. The storm will pass. The spring will come.*
>
> **— Robert H. Schuller**

> *It is difficult for the common good to prevail against the intense concentration of those who have a special interest, especially if the decisions are made behind locked doors.*
>
> **— Jimmy Carter**

> *It is especially important to know who you are. To make decisions. To show who you are.*
>
> **— Malala Yousafzai**

> *I am always wary of decisions made hastily. I am always wary of the first decision, that is, the first thing that comes to my mind if I must decide. This is usually the wrong thing. I have to wait and assess, looking deep into myself, taking the necessary time.*
>
> **— Pope Francis**

> *Making good decisions is a crucial skill at every level.*
>
> **— Peter Drucker**

I think that we must find some way to get more common sense, more rationality, in our decisions and less emotion.

— David Packard

All our final decisions are made in a state of mind that is not going to last.

— Marcel Proust

Exceptionally hard decisions can deplete your energy to the point at which you finally cave in. If you mentally crumble and degenerate into negative thinking, you'll magnify the problem to the point where it can haunt you.

— John C. Maxwell

At the essence of the American presidency is decision-making. Nothing may be more important than a president's ability to make good decisions. They shape history, bring us war or peace, economic growth or stagnation. Presidential choices impact the nation for generations. The style, skill, and experience a candidate has in making decisions should factor heavily in our choice for our country's highest office.

THE OLD BULL DOG ON THE RIGHT TRACK.

Lincoln selecting General Grant, "The Old Bull Dog,"
after relieving General McClellan, courtesy of Library of Congress

The Presidency: The Buck Stops Here

Abraham Lincoln was in the telegraph room of the White House nearly every day. There, he got the latest information on the battles won and lost in the Civil War. He asked questions, searched for data and truth, before making the life and death decisions he constantly faced.

Excellent leaders can simplify a dilemma with evidence.

They are not afraid to decide. Harry Truman said, "The buck stops here."[115]

During the early part of the Obama administration, journalist Jonathan Alter did a study of decision making by President Barack Obama. Alter devoted a considerable amount of time, energy, and research in studying the style of how the new president made decisions. John W. Dean analyzed Alter's findings in a 2010 article for Final Law.[116]

Dean was White House Counsel for President Nixon from 1970 to 1973. He was deeply involved in the events leading up to the Watergate burglary and the coverup. The FBI referred to Dean as the "master manipulator of the coverup." He turned state's evidence and was a key witness for the prosecution. Dean served a reduced prison sentence for his collaboration, which ultimately resulted in the end of the Nixon presidency.[117] Even though Dean was a convicted felon, his time in the Nixon White House gave him some perspective on presidential decision making.

Dean said Obama's style fell between that of George W. Bush and Bill Clinton. Bush had an intuitive style of decision making. It was based on instinct and "gut feel," instead of relying on his Cabinet, staff, and professionals who could provide facts for logical and rational judgements. According to Dean, the result of Bush's way of making decisions led to the disasters in Iraq and Afghanistan and damage to the American economy that may take decades to heal.

---

[115] Emilio Iodice, *Profiles in Leadership: From Caesar to Modern Times*, North American Business Press: Miami, FL, 2013, p. 294

[116] "How Our Decider-in-Chief Decides: Decision Making in the Obama Presidency," John W. Dean, *Final Law*, April 6, 2010 (http://writ.news.findlaw.com/dean/20100806.html); Jonathan Alter, The Promise: President Obama, Year One, Simon and Schuster: New York, 2010

[117] Office of Planning and Evaluation (July 5, 1974), "FBI Watergate Investigation: OPE Analysis" (PDF), Federal Bureau of Investigation, p. 11; File Number 139-4089, retrieved July 19, 2011

"Clinton was an inductive thinker with a horizontal mind. He talked to people in wide-ranging 'college bull sessions' (or late at night on the phone) to establish a broad array of policy and political options, then looked at them in context, and fashioned a synthetic and often brilliant political approach out of the tangled strands of analysis."[118] Obama, instead, made decisions in the same style he used in law school when he headed the Harvard Law Review.

Obama was a "deductive" thinker with a vertical way of reasoning. He reflected profoundly about a subject and fashioned it in a point-by-point series of arguments. He wanted memos that laid out clear policy options. He preferred logic to imagination, in Alter's view. While Clinton constantly reviewed and second- guessed his choices, Obama decided and moved on unless something out of the ordinary required going back to re-evaluate the situation.[119]

He wanted all available data about a subject. He probed his agencies and staffs and "encouraged dissent, rather than yes-people." Obama listened carefully. He repeated what he had heard to make sure he grasped the fundamentals and had interpreted the arguments accurately.

He encouraged his team to think in terms of a larger vision and "the big picture" vs. getting swamped in details. He would change his approach in solving a particular problem so that his staff was kept off-balance and did not tell him what they thought he wanted to hear. Obama did not make-believe he understood when he did not. He asked questions. At the close of a meeting, he summarized what had been said and decided, and then ended the discussion.

Dean and Alter believed the approach Obama followed was an example of the way choices should be made in the White House. Rarely have presidents worked this way, they contended.

John Kennedy failed in making sound decisions in the Bay of Pigs invasion, but he got it right, in their view, during the Cuban Missile Crisis.

---

[118] Ibid. Dean
[119] Ibid. Dean

Dean felt Obama was writing the "textbook" on proper presidential decision-making. Even so, he brought up an important question: Was his style devoid of emotion? He was remarkably cool when tackling crises. He constantly remained self-confident and focused.

Clinton was subject to "purple fits" and tantrums. Bush went with his instincts. Obama acted calmly and logically, according to Dean. He stayed in control of his emotions and, as a result, maintained control of the emotions of those around him. He realized that this was not always the best approach, but he preferred it to any other. Still, Dean believed Obama may be one of our better decision makers, because of his style and fact-based method to tackling difficult choices.

Obama's former CIA Director, Leon Panetta, challenged this view.

Panetta was head of the Central Intelligence Agency from 2009 to 2011. In his book, *Worthy Fights*, he criticized the president's style of making decisions.[120]

Panetta argued against declassifying information related to the Bush era interrogation tactics, for example, and Obama overruled him. Panetta disagreed: "It seemed wrong to me to ask a public servant to take a risk for his country and assure him that it was both legal and approved, then, years later, to suggest that he had done something wrong." Panetta viewed this incident as part of the pattern of how Obama made decisions. In his view, Obama's manner was too "insular."

Decision-making was conducted with the president's inner circle of staffers, often bypassing the Cabinet and the council of senior advisers and experts. The failure to consult specialists, according to Panetta, damaged the administration's ability to explain problems and their solutions. Non-political challenges became political with Obama's form of making decisions. Panetta believed that Obama had a "disdain for Congress," refusing to allow agency heads to deliberate with members.

---

[120] "Panetta's Memoir Blasts Obama On His Leadership, Blames Him for State of Iraq And Syria," by Lauren Walker, *Newsweek*, October 10, 2011

Perhaps Panetta's biggest criticism was the drawdown in Iraq. He insisted that leaving a modest force would preserve stability and reduce the chances of terrorism. The administration wanted to end an unpopular war that they did not support, even if the head of the CIA and the Joint Chiefs of Staff and military commanders felt differently. The resurgence of Al Qaeda, and then ISIS, arose from those critical decisions, in the eyes of administration detractors.

Henry Kissinger being sworn in as Secretary of State by Chief Justice Warren Burger, September 22, 1973. Kissinger's mother, Paula, holds the Bible upon which he was sworn in while President Nixon looks on, courtesy of National Archives

"Mao and Nixon Playing 'Ping Pong Diplomacy,'" 1972, courtesy of Presidency and the Cold War

Another critic was former Defense Secretary Robert Gates. "His White House was by far the most centralized and controlling in national security of any I had seen since Richard Nixon and Henry Kissinger ruled the roost."[121]

Gates wrote in a memoir that he felt "blindsided" at times by decisions made at the White House that affected defense. He considered Obama a man of integrity, but he questioned his ability to make sound judgments regarding national security.

Other presidents faced challenges that required tough decisions that affected our history. Presidents like Adams and Jefferson had fewer staff resources to assist them than modern presidents, but still had to make historic choices.

John Adams, courtesy of the White House

---

[121] Reuters, January 7, 2014, "Former U.S. Defense Secretary Gates criticizes Obama in memoir" (http://www. reuters.com/article/2014/01/08/us-usa-gates-obama-idUSBREA0618020140108)

John Adams: Keeping Us Out of War with France

The second President of the United States, John Adams, was known for his strong personality and independent decision making. Adams was criticized for his temper and demeanor, which could be very argumentative. He admitted that he lacked patience and did not suffer fools silently.[122]

Like his predecessor, George Washington, Adams was considered a patriot of good character and a promoter of republican values. He kept Washington's Cabinet to permit a smoother succession. They were often hostile to his decisions which, at times, he made without consulting them. Thomas Jefferson was Vice President. Adams' Cabinet was led by a team loyal to Alexander Hamilton, who felt a small aristocratic group with ties to England should lead the country, even if it led to war with France. Britain and France were at war. Many Americans recalled that France had helped in the Revolutionary War and were sympathetic to the French. Adams felt that the young republic needed to avoid European entanglements at all costs, even if it meant he would not be re-elected. Adam's self-reliance kept us out of war.

When the French began seizing U.S. merchant vessels, Adams fortified the Navy and defied the French by harassing their vessels on the high seas. He strengthened the army to prevent an invasion. Adams signed the Alien and Sedition Act, which levied penalties on foreigners who spoke out against the government. It angered his political enemies and the public at large. In February 1799, he sent an emissary to France to negotiate with Napoleon. It led to an end to conflict and signaled the start of friendly relations. Even though John Adams avoided war, he lost his bid for re-election.

Adams felt that one of his greatest achievements was keeping America from going to war with France. He asked the following to be written on his tombstone: "Here lies John Adams, who took upon himself the responsibility of peace with France in the year 1800." He and Thomas Jefferson died on the same day, July 4, 1826.[123]

---

[122] George C. Herring, (2008), *From Colony to Superpower: U.S. Foreign Relations Since 1776*, Oxford University Press, p. 91

[123] John McCullough, *John Adams*, Simon & Schuster: 2001, p. 622

Abraham Lincoln, courtesy of Library of Congress

Abraham Lincoln and the Attack on Fort Sumter

As Abraham Lincoln was about to assume office, he faced a crisis beyond expectations. The United States was being torn apart by secessionism. It began on an island in the harbor of Charleston bay. South Carolina seceded from the Union on December 20, 1860. On Christmas day, 68 federal troops stationed in Charleston withdrew to Fort Sumter. The North considered the fort to be federal property. South Carolina insisted that it was part of the newly formed Confederate States of America. In February 1861, Jefferson Davis was inaugurated provisional President of the Confederacy. One month later, Abraham Lincoln took the oath of office.

Fort Sumter, courtesy of Library of Congress

Within weeks, he faced one of the most crucial decisions of his life. Fort Sumter was circled by South Carolina militia. The only way to supply the Fort was by attacking the militia. This would be an act of war and considered Northern aggression. There were Southern states that still had not seceded. If the North liberated the Fort, it might drive other states into the hands of the Confederacy. Foreign powers might take sides to support the South.

At the same time, he could not permit his troops to starve or surrender and risk showing weakness. Lincoln met with his Cabinet advisers and military leaders and studied all options and possible outcomes. He could withdraw the troops from Fort Sumter and negotiate with the South. He could use the Fort to launch an invasion and forcibly bring the South back into the Union. He settled on a middle course that left his options open.

Jefferson Finis Davis, President of the Confederate States, courtesy of National Archives

On April 6, Lincoln sent a message to the governor of South Carolina. He said he would send provisions to Fort Sumter but no arms, troops, or ammunition unless South Carolina attacked. The decision now rested with Jefferson Davis. If the South attacked the Northern troops supplying the Fort, they would be the aggressors. Davis decided he could not permit the Fort to be resupplied. He ordered Major Anderson, the Commander of Fort Sumter, to surrender. He refused. "The Civil War began at 4:30 a.m. on April 12, 1861, when Confederate artillery, under the command of General Pierre Gustave T. Beauregard, opened fire on Fort Sumter. Confederate batteries showered the fort with over 3,000 shells in a three-and-a-half-day period. Anderson surrendered. Ironically, Beauregard had developed his military skills under Anderson's instruction at West Point. This was the first of countless relationships and families devastated in the Civil War. The fight was on."[124]

The attack on Fort Sumter portrayed the North as the victim and not the aggressor. It helped Lincoln rally popular support for what would be the bloodiest conflict in American history.

Woodrow Wilson, courtesy of Library of Congress

---

[124] USHistory.org, Fort Sumter (http://www.ushistory.org/us/33a.asp)

Woodrow Wilson: The Decision to Go to War

"He Kept Us Out of War." This was the slogan that helped re-elect Woodrow Wilson to the White House in 1916. World War I in Europe began two years earlier. The United States declared its neutrality even in the face of unrestricted submarine warfare on the part of Germany. Wilson promised to keep the United States from being entangled in a war that was taking on global proportions. He did not want to be forced to change his stand. A year before the 1916 campaign, an event happened that enraged the American public against Germany.

RMS Lusitania, 1915, courtesy of Library of Congress

The passenger ship, *Lusitania*, set sail on May 1, 1915, from New York bound for Liverpool. It had nearly 2,000 passengers, and it was the fastest ship afloat. The day before it set sail, its captain, William Turner, testified in an ongoing investigation of the sinking of the *Titanic*. He knew details about the treacherous conditions of the Irish Sea and the North Atlantic. What he did not know was that German submarines were prowling the waters in search of British prey.

Below the decks of the *Lusitania* were tons of munitions bound for the United Kingdom.[125] The Admiralty had mounted turrets for guns on the luxury liner. Seven days into its voyage, a German submarine U-20 launched a torpedo. It was 2:10 PM on May 7.

---

[125] The Sinking of the Lusitania (http://www.eyewitnesstohistory.com/snpwwi2.htm)

Two explosions rocked the vessel. The first came from the torpedo, and the second from an unknown source. The ship sank in 18 minutes, with 1,119 passengers dying, including 114 Americans. A firestorm of protests against Germany occurred, and President Wilson sent a strong message to Germany's Kaiser.

Now, U.S. Secretary of State William Jennings Bryan was a pacifist, so he resigned, realizing that war was ahead.

This cartoon, featuring President Woodrow Wilson, was in response to continued German U-boat attacks at sea in World War I (March 21, 1917), courtesy of National Archives

Less than two years later, the Germans attempted an alliance with Mexico that forced Woodrow Wilson to reconsider America's neutrality. British authorities gave the U.S. a telegram from German Foreign Secretary Arthur Zimmerman to the German Ambassador to Mexico. It proposed a German-Mexican alliance in the event of war with the United States. Germany promised Mexico restoration of the territories lost to the US during the Mexican War of 1845.

The telegram appeared on the front pages of newspapers around the world on March 1, 1917.

At first it was suspected of being a hoax.

But two days later, Zimmerman revealed that it was true.

Americans were horrified. Wilson could no longer wait. He had to decide on the only course of action.

On April 2, President Wilson asked Congress for a declaration of war. It was approved four days later. He asked the American people to join the fight "to make the world safe for democracy."

The Manhattan Project

It was August 2, 1939. Albert Einstein was teaching at Princeton University. On that date, he wrote an historic letter to President Franklin Delano Roosevelt one month before the German attack on Poland that started World War II. It would change the course of history.

Albert Einstein, cover of *Time* magazine, 1946, courtesy of *Time*

Einstein wrote to FDR:

"It may become possible to set up a nuclear chain reaction in a large mass of uranium, by which vast amounts of power and large quantities of new radium-like elements would be generated. Now, it appears almost certain that this could be achieved in the immediate future. This new phenomenon would also lead to the construction of bombs, and it is conceivable — though much less certain — that extremely powerful bombs of a new type may thus be constructed. A single bomb of this type, carried by boat and exploded in a port, might very well destroy the whole port, together with some of the surrounding territory."

Einstein ended his letter by saying that Germany could be in the process of constructing the same weapon. Years later, Einstein would lament the decision to write the letter. He was a pacifist and hated war. He justified it on the fact that Hitler was advancing in his research and might be able to make the bomb before America. He knew it could destroy the world.

The first test of an atom bomb conducted at New Mexico's Alamogordo Bombing and Gunnery Range on 16 July 1945, courtesy of National Archives

Roosevelt took Einstein's letter seriously and appointed a secret commission to study the feasibility of the project. Once it was clear that the atomic bomb could be made, FDR decided to move forward. On October 9, 1941, less than two months before Pearl Harbor, the president gave the authority and responsibility to Vannevar Bush, head of the National Defense Research Committee, to do all that was necessary to create the first nuclear device to be used in warfare.

Franklin Roosevelt sitting alone in the White House, 1941, courtesy of National Archives

Roosevelt made his choice only in the presence of Bush and Vice President Henry Wallace, and no one else. He did not bring in other members of his administration or the Congress. He felt that the level of secrecy was so important that the responsibility and the decision should be his, and his alone. It was the largest secret project ever undertaken by the United States.

FDR told Bush to proceed aggressively and spend whatever was necessary to achieve the goal of producing the first atomic bomb. By the time it was completed, 130,000 people were employed on the Manhattan Project. It cost $2 billion at the time, which is equivalent to nearly $30 billion today.

President Franklin Roosevelt addressing a joint session of Congress on
December 8, 1941, asking for a Declaration of War against Japan,
courtesy of Library of Congress

Franklin Delano Roosevelt and the Attack on Pearl Harbor

On December 7, 1941, the Japanese attacked Pearl Harbor, in Hawaii.
President Franklin Roosevelt had to immediately sort out conflicting
and inaccurate information to understand the details of the attack,
the loss of life, and the impact on the U.S. Navy. More importantly, he
prepared his address to Congress to ask for a Declaration of War
against the Empire of Japan.

FDR in 1942, at age 60, at the start of World War II, courtesy of Aunt Ethel's War

Franklin Roosevelt had assembled a splendid Cabinet of hard working, dedicated officials who were experts in their fields. Without consulting his team, FDR decided on a short message mentioning only Japan. His senior foreign policy and military advisers wanted a long explanation to demonstrate how the United States had done everything possible to preserve peace. They wanted him to declare war on Germany and Italy, as well. His Cabinet officers were unanimously opposed to Roosevelt's brief address. They discussed and argued the issue into the night.

Secretary of State Cordell Hull insisted that "the most important war in 500 years deserved more than a short statement." Secretary of War Henry Stimson added that "Germany had inspired and planned this whole affair and that the President should so state in his message." Hull pressed the president to give a detailed address that would demonstrate the history of "Japan's lawless conduct," and connect the attack on Pearl Harbor to the Nazis. Stimson agreed.[126] Franklin Roosevelt rejected their recommendations.

He trusted his instincts, which were usually correct. His goal was to speak to the American people. They would be listening to his every word on the radio.

It was the people who counted.

He was asking them to send their children to fight and die. The President was also concerned about giving the enemy too much information about the extent of the attack on Pearl Harbor. He did not want to ask for a declaration of war against Germany and Italy at that moment. FDR understood public opinion. Polls indicated that a conflict with Japan was more popular than one with the other Axis powers.

Franklin Roosevelt was right, and he had the strength to overrule his Secretaries of War, State, and the Navy. He followed his strategic sense of what was right and wrong. At the time, there were no instant surveys or round the clock TV coverage to truly and accurately tell him the national mood.

---

[126] Steven M. Gillon, Scholar-in-Residence at History and Professor of History at the University of Oklahoma (http://www.huffingtonpost.com/steven-m-gillon/fdr-pearl-harbor_b_1115034.html)

If he had followed the suggestions of his Cabinet, there would be no "Day of Infamy" speech, which is one of the greatest examples of presidential oratory and leadership in American history.[127]

> *"Yesterday, December 7, 1941. . . a date which will live in infamy, the United States of America was suddenly and deliberately attacked by naval and air forces of the Empire of Japan . . . . With confidence in our armed forces, with the unbounding determination of our people, we will gain the inevitable triumph — so help us God."*

— Franklin Roosevelt's Speech to Congress, December 8, 1941

Franklin Roosevelt signing Declaration of War
against Japan, December 8, 1941, courtesy of Library of Congress

Evacuation of Japanese Americans from West Coast areas
under U.S. Army War Emergency Order, 1942, courtesy of Library of Congress

---

[127] Gillon

The Internment of Japanese Americans

After the Japanese attack on Pearl Harbor, the U.S. moved rapidly to prepare for the war effort, militarily and domestically. President Roosevelt faced the dilemma of dealing with a two-front conflict, one in the Far East and one in Europe. He also had to deal with the fate of Japanese Americans who lived on the West Coast of the United States.

There were hundreds of thousands of them.

Many were second and third generation Americans. Their loyalties were challenged. "The Japanese race is an enemy race," wrote Lt. Gen. John DeWitt, the man in charge of the Western Defense Command. And while many second- and third-generation Japanese born on United States soil, possessed of United States citizenship, have become 'Americanized,' the racial strains are undiluted."[128]

Attorney General Francis Biddle and Army Deputy Chief of Staff Mark Clark were against internment of the Japanese. FDR believed he was protecting the homeland from espionage. He feared that the loyalties of Japanese Americans would lean more toward Japan than toward the United States.

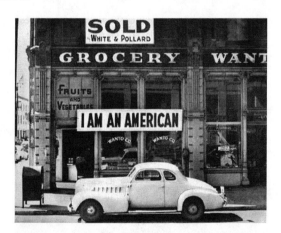

A store owner's response to anti-Japanese sentiment in the wake of the Pearl Harbor attack, Oakland, Calif., 1942, courtesy of National Archives

---

[128] The War, Civil Rights, Japanese Americans (http://www.pbs.org/thewar/at_home_civil_rights_japanese_american.htm)

The president signed Executive Order 9066 on February 19, 1942. It authorized the military to remove anyone from any part of the country that they believed was a threat to national security.

More than 110,000 Japanese Americans were rounded up and shipped to camps in Wyoming, Arkansas, and Arizona. Thousands of Italian and German aliens would also be interred, although millions of citizens who were from Germany or Italy remained free to live normal lives.

It was the Japanese who were singled out.

"It took no great effort of imagination to see the hatred of many Americans for the enemy turned on us, who looked so much like him," observed Senator Daniel Inouye, who was 17 years old at the time. His life and that of his family was swept up in the aftermath of FDR's decision.[129] The injustice perpetrated against Japanese Americans during World War II is an example of how the government can abridge constitutional liberties in times of emergencies, with terrible results.[130]

Twenty-five years after WWII ended, the U.S. Congress set up a commission to investigate the legacy of the camps. Interviews and testimonies were gathered. The commission's final report called the incarceration a "grave injustice" motivated by "racial prejudice, war hysteria, and the failure of political leadership."[131]

President Ronald Reagan signing the Civil Liberties Act of 1988,
August 10, 1988, Washington, D.C., courtesy of National Archives

---

[129] The War, Civil Rights, Japanese Americans (http://www.pbs.org/thewar/at_home_civil_rights_japanese_american.htm)
[130] Ibid.
[131] Personal Justice Denied, June 1983, Report of the Commission on Wartime Internment of Civilians (http://www.archives.gov/research/japanese-americans/justice-denied/part-2-recommendations.pdf)

In 1988, Ronald Reagan signed the Civil Liberties Act to compensate more than 100,000 people of Japanese descent who were incarcerated in the camps. The law offered a formal apology and monetary compensation to survivors. It was approved by Congress after a decade-long fight by the Japanese American community.[132]

Harry Truman: Judgment at Nuremberg

If we do not learn from history, we are doomed to repeat it.

— George Santayana

We must work to bind up the wounds of a suffering world—to build an abiding peace, a peace rooted in justice and in law. We can build such a peace only by hard, toilsome, painstaking work—by understanding and working with our allies in peace as we have in war.

— Harry Truman

It was the afternoon of April 12, 1945. That day, the Vice President presided over the Senate, as usual.

Harry Truman had replaced Vice President Henry Wallace on the ticket for 1944. The party wanted someone strong to help win the election. They also knew that Franklin Roosevelt was dying. Wallace was considered too far to the left to take on the role of Chief Executive. Truman was a compromise candidate who had worked to pass New Deal legislation. He was considered honest and tough.

---

[132] Ibid. Personal Justice Denied

President Roosevelt, Vice President-elect Truman and Vice President Wallace,
November 10, 1944, after the Democratic ticket's election victory,
courtesy of National Archives

It was customary for Truman and House Speaker Sam Rayburn to have their traditional drink of bourbon and water after a long day of Senate proceedings. Suddenly, the Vice President was called to the phone. It was Steve Early, President Roosevelt's chief spokesperson. He asked him to come to the White House, immediately. The Vice President expected that he would be given some important legislative mission.

In FDR's private quarters, he found himself with the First Lady. "Harry, the President is dead," said Eleanor Roosevelt. Truman was shocked. "Is there anything I can do for you?" he asked. "Is there anything we can do for you, Harry?" she responded. "For you are the one in trouble now."[133]

Truman said later that he felt he had "been struck by a bolt of lightning ... and that the moon, the stars and the planets had all fallen on me ... I felt as if I had lived five lifetimes in those first days as President."

Truman had been Vice President 82 days.

He met Roosevelt twice during that time, yet he was uninformed about the major events concerning the war and the administration's post-war plans.

---

133 "Eleanor and Harry: The Correspondence of Eleanor Roosevelt and Harry S. Truman," Harry S. Truman Library & Museum, retrieved July 28, 2012

Harry Truman was frightened.

He knew he was no Franklin Roosevelt. He was not charismatic and had a fragile ego, which few observers could perceive. Unlike FDR, he did not have a political streak, and he had not developed the skill to manipulate others to gain leverage. Truman was direct and considered himself a straight shooter who made decisions based on facts. He realized that the best way to gain trust with the people was to move forward aggressively to fulfill FDR's wartime and post-wartime programs.

The new commander-in-chief needed to show vigor and activism, and he did.

Truman asked Roosevelt's Cabinet to remain in place. He said he would listen to their advice, but he would be the one making the decisions that he expected them to support. The new President immediately set out to make difficult choices to deal with ending the war and the reconstruction of Europe and Japan. *The New York Times* described it this way:

"In war-ravaged Europe in those years, Truman and the United States established peace and held back Soviet expansion and built economic and political stability through the Truman Doctrine, the Marshall Plan, and the North Atlantic Treaty Organization. In the Mideast, he recognized the State of Israel. In the Far East, the President imposed peace and constitutional democracy on the Japanese enemy, tried valiantly to save China from Communism, and chose to wage war in Korea to halt aggression. In the United States, Truman led the nation's conversion from war to peace, while maintaining a stable and prosperous economy."[134]

---

[134] Alden Whitman, "Harry S. Truman: Decisive President," New York Times, December 27, 1972 (http://www.nytimes.com/learning/general/onthisday/bday/0508.html)

One of the most critical decisions facing Truman was the trial of Nazis accused of war crimes. In 1943, Roosevelt, Stalin, and Churchill met in Tehran. Stalin wanted summary executions of German officers. Churchill disagreed and called for trials of those involved in crimes against humanity. Secretary of War Henry Stimson was charged with coming up with a plan for trying the Nazis at the end of the war. The resulting plan was titled, "Trial of European War Criminals." As the war progressed toward a conclusion, the Allies were unable to come to grips with whether to hold the trials at all or to conduct summary executions.

The proposal to proceed or not was presented to President Truman. The Chief Justice of the U.S. Supreme Court, Harlan Fiske Stone, and Justice William O. Douglas were opposed to the trials. Stone accused the Chief Prosecutor of conducting "a high-grade lynching party."[135] Truman was not swayed by opposition to the trials. Jeffrey Lawrence, the chief British Judge at the Nuremberg Tribunal, summed up the situation:

---

[135] *Dönitz at Nuremberg: A Reappraisal*, H. K. Thompson, Jr., and Henry Strutz, Inst. for Historical Review (Torrance, Calif.: 1983)

"There were, I suppose, three possible courses: to let the atrocities which had been committed go unpunished; to put the perpetrators to death or punish them by executive action; or to try them. Which was it to be? Was it possible to let such atrocities go unpunished? Could France, could Russia, could Holland, Belgium, Norway, Czechoslovakia, Poland, or Yugoslavia be expected to consent to such a course? ... It will be remembered that after the First World War, alleged criminals were handed over to be tried by Germany, and what a farce that was! The majority got off and such sentences as were inflicted were derisory and were soon remitted."[136]

On May 2, 1945, President Truman appointed Robert H. Jackson, Associate Justice of the Supreme Court of the United States, to lead the prosecution of the chief Nazi warlords at the Nuremberg Tribunal. Truman gave Jackson free rein to choose his team and represent the United States at the trial. Jackson worked to achieve a consensus among the Allies, which was called the London Charter. It became the basis for the proceedings before the International Military Tribunal. It lasted ten months. Among the twenty-two defendants were Hermann Goering, President of the Reichstag, and Albert Speer, Minister of Armaments and War Production.

The defendants at Nuremberg, courtesy of National Archives

[136] Lawrence, 1947, pp. 152-3; this speech by Lawrence is reprinted in Mettraux, 2008, pp. 290-9

The trial opened on November 19, 1945. The indictments against 24 major war criminals and seven organizations, which included the Nazi Party, the Reich Court, and the General Staff and High Command of Germany, were for:[137]

1. Participation in a common plan or conspiracy for the accomplishment of a crime against peace

2. Planning, initiating, and waging wars of aggression and other crimes against peace

3. War crimes

4. Crimes against humanity

"It was the first time an international tribunal had sought to sentence the leaders of a regime — politicians, army officers, and economic advisors — even though in some cases direct responsibility for specific criminal acts could not be attributed to them.

"As a group, they were initiators, aides, organizers, and executers of crimes against humanity. They were accused of orchestrating wars of aggression, murdering civilians and prisoners of war, deporting people, plundering, engaging in racial persecution, murdering European Jews, and occupying numerous European countries."[138]

On October 1, 1946, the verdict was rendered. Three of the defendants were acquitted, four sentenced to prison terms from 10 to 20 years, three sentenced to life imprisonment, and twelve were sentenced to death by hanging. Ten of the condemned Nazi criminals were executed two weeks later. Goering escaped his fate by taking a cyanide capsule hours before his execution.

---

[137] Henkel (ed.), Matthias (2011), "Memoriam Nuernberger Prozesse," exhibition catalogue (German), Nuremberg: Museen der Stadt Nuernberg, 78 pp
[138] "Nuremberg Trials Left a Lasting Legacy" (http://www.dw.com/en/nuremberg-trials-left-a-lasting-legacy/a-6237501)

The American authorities conducted subsequent Nuremberg Trials in their occupied zone. Other trials conducted after the Nuremberg Trials include the following:[139]

- Auschwitz Trial
- Belsen Trial
- Belzec Trial, before the 1st Munich District Court in the mid-1960s, of eight SS-men of the Belzec extermination camp
- Chełmno trials of the Chełmno extermination camp personnel, held in Poland and in Germany; the cases were decided almost twenty years apart
- Dachau Trials
- Frankfurt Auschwitz Trials
- Majdanek trials; the longest Nazi war crimes trial in history, spanning over 30 years
- Mauthausen-Gusen camp trials
- Ravensbrück Trial
- Sobibor trial held in Hagen, Germany, in 1965 against the SS-men of the Sobibor extermination camp
- Treblinka trials in Düsseldorf, Germany

The legacy of the Nuremberg Trials led to the adoption by the United Nations affirming "the principles in international law recognized by the Charter of the Nuremberg Tribunal and by the judgement of the Tribunal." In 1950, the International Law Commission submitted seven principles to the U.N. as the basis of a code of crimes against humanity that are still in effect today.

As he announced the end of the War in Europe, President Truman expressed his feelings that coincided with his decision about Nuremberg:

---

[139] Kevin Jon Heller (2011), *The Trials. Introduction: The indictments, biographical information, and the verdicts. The Nuremberg Military Tribunals and the Origins of International Criminal Law*, Oxford University Press: pp. 85–; retrieved 10 January 2015

"Our rejoicing is sobered and subdued by a supreme consciousness of the terrible price we have paid to rid the world of Hitler and his evil band. Let us not forget, my fellow Americans, the sorrow and the heartache which today abide in the homes of so many of our neighbors—neighbors whose most priceless possession has been rendered as a sacrifice to redeem our liberty."

During the commemoration of the seventieth anniversary of the liberation of Auschwitz, a member of the Canadian Parliament, Irwin Cotler, said these words:[140]

"Finally, we must remember – and celebrate – the survivors of the Holocaust, the true heroes of humanity. For they witnessed and endured the worst of inhumanity, but somehow found, in the depths of their own humanity, the courage to go on, to rebuild their lives as they helped build our communities.

"And so, together with them we must remember and pledge – not as an idle slogan but as an injunction to act — that never again will we be indifferent to incitement and hate, never again will we be silent in the face of evil, never again will we indulge racism and anti-Semitism, never again will we ignore the plight of the vulnerable, and never again will we be indifferent in the face of mass atrocity and impunity.

"We will speak up and act against racism, against hate, against anti-Semitism, against mass atrocity, against injustice, and against the crime of crimes whose name we should shudder to mention: genocide."

---

[140] Irwin Cotler, "70 years later: Universal lessons for our time," *The Jerusalem Post*, January 29, 2015 (http://www.jpost.com/Opinion/70-years-later-Universal-lessons-for-our-time-389450)

The Decision to Drop the Atomic Bomb

Atomic bombs over Hiroshima and Nagasaki, August 1945, courtesy of National Archives

Harry Truman, courtesy of National Archives

Franklin Delano Roosevelt died on April 12, 1945. Harry Truman was sworn in the same day.

As noted, he had been Vice President for eighty-two days. He had met with FDR twice since inauguration day on January 20. He knew that a weapon capable of mass destruction had been developed and that it could bring a sudden end to the war with Japan. When President Truman learned of the Manhattan Project, he realized he faced a decision that no President of the United States had ever encountered.

Ending the war with Japan was in his grasp.

Raising the flag at Iwo Jima, courtesy of National Archives

It could save the lives of hundreds of thousands of American soldiers and sailors who would be forced to invade Japan to compel the Japanese to surrender. At the same time, it would unleash the most terrible weapon ever conceived.

Americans were exhausted from four years of war in Europe and the Pacific. Over 150,000 Japanese and Allied personnel died in the taking of Okinawa, alone. It was the bloodiest battle of the Pacific war and had a profound influence on President Truman and his decision to use the atomic bomb to bring about the surrender of Japan.

Japanese cities were being firebombed. Despite the relentless destruction, the Japanese military refused to give up. An army of two million soldiers were prepared to defend the Japanese homeland. Truman had to decide to either use the bomb or conduct one of the longest and bloodiest invasions in history. He consulted with officers, scientists, and diplomats to determine the best course of action.

The U.S. military estimated that an amphibious landing could result in a million Allied casualties and, perhaps, the death of millions of Japanese.

President Truman had to weigh the cost in American lives, as well as enemy lives. He felt that using the bomb would end the war and save suffering on both sides. Continuing the war was not really an option. Over 3,500 Japanese kamikaze raids had produced extensive loss of American military personnel and great destruction.

Truman rejected the idea of a demonstration bomb to shake the Japanese military into submission. There was no certainty that they would capitulate, even if the test succeeded. And a failed test would be making matters worse than no test at all.

President Truman believed that the new weapon would act like the massive fire-bombing of Tokyo or Dresden. The scientific community did not foresee the immense effects of radiation poisoning. The President decided to use the first nuclear weapon to bring an end to the overwhelming bloodshed of the war.

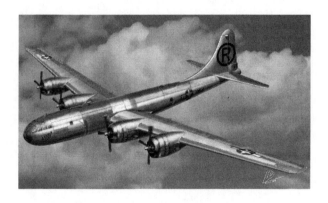

The plane that dropped the first atomic bombs,
The Enola Gay, August 1945, courtesy of National Archives

On August 6, 1945, the first atomic blast occurred over the city of Hiroshima. Within minutes, 70,000 Japanese citizens were vaporized. Another 100,000 died in the months and years to come, from radiation sickness.

And the Empire of Japan refused to lay down its military arms.

A second nuclear device was unleashed three days later on Nagasaki. 80,000 people died instantly.[141] The nuclear age was born, along with the possibility of atomic war.

> The atomic bomb made the prospect of future war unendurable. It has led us up those last few steps to the mountain pass; and beyond there is a different country.

> — **J. Robert Oppenheimer**

> As human beings, our greatness lies not so much in being able to remake the world — that is the myth of the atomic age — as in being able to remake ourselves.

> — **Mahatma Gandhi**

Thoughts Over the Use of the Atomic Bomb to End the War with Japan

> There are voices which assert that the bomb should never have been used at all. I cannot associate myself with such ideas. . . . I am surprised that very worthy people—but people who in most cases had no intention of proceeding to the Japanese front themselves—should adopt the position that rather than throw this bomb, we should have sacrificed a million American and a quarter of a million British lives.

> — **Winston Churchill**

> But they (the Japanese) also showed a meanness and viciousness towards their enemies equal to the Huns. Genghis Khan and his hordes could not have been more merciless. I have no doubts about whether the two atom bombs dropped on Hiroshima and Nagasaki were necessary. Without them, hundreds of thousands of civilians in Malaya and Singapore, and millions in Japan itself, would have perished.

> — **Lee Kuan Yew, Former Prime Minister of Singapore**

---

[141] UShistory.org, "The Decision to Drop the Atom Bomb" (http://www.ushistory.org/us/51g.asp)

The intercepts of Japanese Imperial Army and Navy messages disclosed without exception that Japan's armed forces were determined to fight a final Armageddon battle in the homeland against an Allied invasion. The Japanese called this strategy Ketsu Go (Operation Decisive). It was founded on the premise that American morale was brittle and could be shattered by heavy losses in the initial invasion. American politicians would then gladly negotiate an end to the war far more generous than unconditional surrender.

— Richard B. Frank, Historian

The Japanese code of Bushido—'the way of the warrior'—was deeply ingrained. The concept of Yamato-damashii equipped each soldier with a strict code: Never be captured, never break down, and never surrender. Surrender was dishonorable. Each soldier was trained to fight to the death and was expected to die before suffering dishonor. Defeated Japanese leaders preferred to take their own lives in the painful samurai ritual of seppuku (called hara kiri in the West). Warriors who surrendered were deemed not worthy of regard or respect.

— John T. Correll

Much of the confusion involves the definition of terms like 'surrender.' The Japanese did indeed float various schemes to end the war, but on terms that were totally unacceptable to any Allied power. Among other things, these schemes involved no occupation, no dismantling of militarism or imperialism, and no punishment of war criminals. No retaliation for the savage crimes in China, the East Indies, and elsewhere. Then, after a hiatus of a couple years, Japan would launch the next wave of aggression. They were clearly not talking 'surrender' in any sense of the term we might recognize …. When we consider the toll of not dropping the bombs, always remember the many thousands of civilians who were dying under Japanese occupation in China and Indonesia throughout 1945, and we should continue counting the deaths that would have occurred at that rate through 1946. Nothing was going to stop that short of the total destruction of Japanese war-making capacity.

Add to this the murder of all Allied POWs in Japanese hands, as the Japanese had ordered in the event of a direct attack on the mainland. Put those figures together, together with likely Japanese fatalities, you get about ten million dead — and that is a conservative figure. The vast majority of those additional deaths would have been East and Southeast Asians, mainly Japanese and Chinese.

— **Philip Jenkins**

In 1945, Secretary of War Stimson, visiting my headquarters in Germany, informed me that our government was preparing to drop an atomic bomb on Japan. I was one of those who felt that there were a number of cogent reasons to question the wisdom of such an act. During his recitation of the relevant facts, I had been conscious of a feeling of depression, and so I voiced to him my grave misgivings, first on the basis of my belief that Japan was already defeated and that dropping the bomb was completely unnecessary, and secondly because I thought that our country should avoid shocking world opinion by the use of a weapon whose employment was, I thought, no longer mandatory as a measure to save American lives.

— **Dwight David Eisenhower**

The Japanese had, in fact, already sued for peace. The atomic bomb played no decisive part, from a purely military point of view, in the defeat of Japan.

— *Fleet Admiral Chester W. Nimitz, Commander in Chief of the U.S. Pacific Fleet*

The use of [the atomic bombs] at Hiroshima and Nagasaki was of no material assistance in our war against Japan. The Japanese were already defeated and ready to surrender because of the effective sea blockade and the successful bombing with conventional weapons. . . . The lethal possibilities of atomic warfare in the future are frightening. My own feeling was that in being the first to use it, we had adopted an ethical standard common to the barbarians of the Dark Ages. I was not taught to make war in that fashion, and wars cannot be won by destroying women and children.

— Fleet Admiral William D. Leahy, Chief of Staff to President Truman, 1950

The atomic bomb had nothing to do with the end of the war at all.

— Major General Curtis LeMay, XXI Bomber Command, September 1945

The first atomic bomb was an unnecessary experiment . . . . It was a mistake to ever drop it . . . . [the scientists] had this toy and they wanted to try it out, so they dropped it.

— Fleet Admiral William Halsey Jr., 1946

On the basis of available evidence, however, it is clear that the two atomic bombs . . . alone were not decisive in inducing Japan to surrender. Despite their destructive power, the atomic bombs were not sufficient to change the direction of Japanese diplomacy. The Soviet invasion was. Without the Soviet entry in the war, the Japanese would have continued to fight until numerous atomic bombs, a successful allied invasion of the home islands, or continued aerial bombardments, combined with a naval blockade, rendered them incapable of doing so.

— Tsuyoshi Hasegawa, Japanese Historian

Military vulnerability, not civilian vulnerability, accounts for Japan's decision to surrender. Japan's military position was so poor that its leaders would likely have surrendered before invasion, and at roughly the same time in August 1945, even if the United States had not employed strategic bombing or the atomic bomb. Rather than concern for the costs and risks to the population, or even Japan's overall military weakness vis-a-vis the United States, the decisive factor was Japanese leaders' recognition that their strategy for holding the most important territory at issue—the home islands—could not succeed.

— Robert Pape

Let me say only this much to the moral issue involved: Suppose Germany had developed two bombs before we had any bombs. And suppose Germany had dropped one bomb, say, on Rochester and the other on Buffalo, and then having run out of bombs she would have lost the war. Can anyone doubt that we would then have defined the dropping of atomic bombs on cities as a war crime, and that we would have sentenced the Germans who were guilty of this crime to death at Nuremberg and hanged them?

— Leó Szilárd, physicist who played a role in the Manhattan Project

The Firing of General Douglas MacArthur

General Douglas MacArthur, in the Philippines ,1944, courtesy of National Archives

Douglas MacArthur was one of the most celebrated and popular generals in American history. He was the former Superintendent of the U.S. Military Academy at West Point; among the youngest major generals in Army history; Military Advisor to the Commonwealth Government of the Philippines; Commander of the U.S. Army forces in the Far East; Supreme Commander of the Southwestern Pacific forces; presided over the Japanese surrender in World War II; oversaw the occupation of Japan; and received the Congressional Medal of Honor.

War broke out in Korea in 1950 when North Korea invaded South Korea. MacArthur was called back to head up United Nations forces. At the beginning of the conflict, MacArthur had prepared some brilliant strategies that saved the South from falling into the hands of communist forces from the North. MacArthur pushed for a policy to invade the North.

Truman and MacArthur meeting in South Korea, courtesy of National Archives

President Truman accepted the plan, but he was concerned that Communist China could enter the conflict. MacArthur met with Truman in October 1950 and assured him that the chances of China entering the war were slim. A month later, hundreds of thousands of Chinese soldiers hurled themselves against American forces driving them back into the South. MacArthur asked permission to bomb China. Truman refused. He did not want to expand the conflict. His goal was to limit the communist advance and save South Korea from being taken over by the North.

The Outcome of the Firing of General MacArthur, courtesy of National Archives

MacArthur disagreed publicly with the president. He made a series of statements that bordered on insubordination. President Truman had to assert the authority of his office and his civilian authority over the military. Truman's standing in the polls and his popularity with the public was one of the lowest for any president. This had no effect on his decision. Truman listened to his Secretary of Defense, George Marshall, and his Secretary of State, Dean Acheson. They told the president that firing MacArthur would provoke a firestorm in the press and with the public. He listened to his team, but kept his own counsel.

President Truman knew the political consequences of his decision.

He knew it would hurt him and his party in the elections of 1952. Even so, he knew what the proper choice to make was. On April 11, 1951, General Douglas MacArthur, hero of World War II and one of the most popular military figures in American history, was relieved of his command.

Paul Loring, 1951, courtesy of *The Providence Evening Bulletin*

He returned to the United States to a welcome befitting a great hero. A ticker tape parade in New York and parades and ceremonies elsewhere marked the end of a magnificent career. MacArthur addressed a joint session of Congress. His farewell address received fifty standing ovations. He defended his actions in Korea and his disagreement with the President. He ended his speech with these words:[142]

---

[142] Torricelli, Robert G., Andrew Carroll, and Doris Kearns Goodwin, *In Our Own Words: Extraordinary Speeches of the American Century,* Washington Square Press: 2008, pp.185-188, ISBN: 978-0-7434-1052-6, OCLC 45144217

I am closing my 52 years of military service. When I joined the Army, even before the turn of the century, it was the fulfillment of all my boyish hopes and dreams. The world has turned over many times since I took the oath on the plain at West Point, and the hopes and dreams have long since vanished, but I still remember the refrain of one of the most popular barrack ballads of that day, which proclaimed most proudly that "old soldiers never die; they just fade away."

And like the old soldier of that ballad, I now close my military career and just fade away, an old soldier who tried to do his duty as God gave him the light to see that duty. Goodbye.

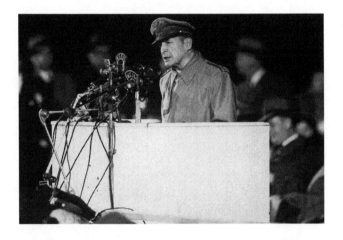

MacArthur speaking at Soldier Field in Chicago, 1951, courtesy of National Archives

There will be moments when the head of the nation will have to make crucial decisions. The legacy of the decisions of FDR and Truman, for example, are still with us today. We must remember that the Commander in Chief must make choices that will affect our children and grandchildren, and their children.

One's philosophy is not best expressed in words; it is expressed in the choices one makes ... and the choices we make are ultimately our responsibility.

— **Eleanor Roosevelt**

Every person has free choice. Free to obey or disobey the Natural Laws. Your choice determines the consequences. Nobody ever did, or ever will, escape the consequences of his choices.

— Alfred A. Montapert

It is our choices . . . that show what we truly are, far more than our abilities.

— J. K. Rowling

We must make the choices that enable us to fulfill the deepest capacities of our real selves.

— Thomas Merton

You are doomed to make choices. This is life's greatest paradox.

— Wayne Dyer

There are two primary choices in life: to accept conditions as they exist, or accept the responsibility for changing them.

— Denis Waitley

PART TWO: Leadership Qualities of The Commander in Chief
CHAPTER TEN:
Humility

It was pride that changed angels into devils; it is humility that makes men as angels.

— Saint Augustine

We come nearest to the great when we are great in humility.

— R. Ta

Pride makes us artificial... humility makes us real.

— Thomas Merton

The principles of living greatly include the capacity to face trouble with courage, disappointment with cheerfulness, and trial with humility.

— Thomas S. Monson

Humility is the true key to success. Successful people lose their way at times. They often embrace and overindulge from the fruits of success. Humility halts this arrogance and self-indulging trap. Humble people share the credit and wealth, remaining focused and hungry to continue the journey of success.

— Rick Pitino

A grateful heart is a beginning of greatness. It is an expression of humility. It is a foundation for the development of such virtues as prayer, faith, courage, contentment, happiness, love, and well-being.

— James E. Faust

There is no respect for others without humility in one's self.

— Henri Frederic Amiel

The first test of a truly great man is his humility. By humility I don't mean doubt of his powers or hesitation in speaking his opinion, but merely an understanding of the relationship of what he can say and what he can do.

— John Ruskin

A president or prime minister without humility will not survive.

Their office requires a humble occupant who is willing to learn and admit what they do not know.

Humility allows them to listen.

It gives them the temperament to admit mistakes without appearing weak. It demands that they consult with experts and pick leaders for their team who may be perceived as being superior, but can get the job done.

A president who builds a strong 'brain trust' of the best and the brightest will need to deal with extraordinary individuals who are professionals and will know more than they do.

Humility to listen and learn, matched with self-confidence that is not arrogance, is the key formula to tackling great challenges.

It allows dissenters and advocates to have their say without worrying about the consequences. They know that the president is searching for facts, solutions, and will tolerate disagreements if they stress problems and not personalities.

The president that stands out above all others for having been both humble and immensely successful was Abraham Lincoln.

Abraham Lincoln, courtesy of Library of Congress

The Humility of Abraham Lincoln

The humility of Abe Lincoln that he carried into the White House came from his modest beginnings and the enormous sense of empathy he had for others and for the world around him, and for being unconventional for his times.

He grew up on the prairie, where men were measured by their ability to hunt, farm, drink, and smoke, and how harshly they treated women. Lincoln was a teetotaler; he loved animals, and he was almost a vegetarian.

He did not smoke, drink, or chew tobacco.

In 1836, he advocated for women's right to vote.

Abraham Lincoln was by no means politically correct for his times. Yet within his differences was a sense of self-worth and respect for all creation and all human beings.

Lincoln was a man who had more failures than successes in life. It was those setbacks that contributed to his humility and his ability to understand that each person is fighting their own battle for survival. He was rejected twice by women he loved. His marriage to Mary Todd was not an easy one. They had four sons. Edward died when he was four. Willie died at twelve and Tad at eighteen. The loss of their children was impossible to forget for Mary and Abraham. He suffered from sadness and, some claim, clinical depression for most of his life.

He was not a success in business. He failed at his first bid for elected office. Later, he served four terms in the Illinois legislature, being elected to the House of Representatives in 1846. He supported Zachary Taylor for President. Lincoln hoped to be appointed Commissioner of the General Land Office. The job went to a rival. He went back to practicing law.

He lost his Senate bid to Stephen Douglas in 1858. Despite professional setbacks and personal heartbreaks, he never gave up. Two years after losing the race for the Senate, he was elected President. He was not his party's first choice. There were other candidates who had more experience in Washington politics, like New York Governor William H. Seward, Congressman Edward Bates, and well-known attorney Salmon P. Chase. Lincoln was being positioned as a second choice if the leading candidates fell.

Against these distinguished leaders, a nearly unknown "prairie lawyer" and one-term Congressman was chosen as the presidential candidate of the Republican Party in 1860. After the election, Lincoln would select these men, his "team of rivals," to help him govern. Edwin Stanton, a man he knew as a lawyer, was chosen to be Secretary of War. Lincoln met him when they pleaded a case together. Stanton did not like him, and Lincoln knew this. He even said derogatory things about him. This did not faze Lincoln. He saw in Stanton the toughness, integrity and determination needed to harness the military might of the nation to fight the Civil War.

A cartoon in 1864, taking a swing at Lincoln's Administration, featuring Lincoln,
William Fessenden, Edwin Stanton, William Seward, and Gideon Welles

In the beginning, the choice of Stanton appeared a mistake. He
continued his condescending ways. At times, it seemed that the
Secretary of War was working at cross purposes to the president.
Stanton disobeyed Lincoln when he felt he was wrong. Stanton's
attitude did not affect Lincoln. He forcefully corrected him to set the
record straight and make sure his decisions were followed. He rarely
took offense, even at the gravest insults. Lincoln focused on the big
picture—winning the war.

If his Cabinet liked him was of little concern to Abraham Lincoln, his
preoccupation was their doing their job well and preserving the Union,
which was his vision and his goal.

> One day, a Congressman arrived at Lincoln's office, reporting that the
> Secretary of War had not only countermanded a direct order from
> Lincoln, but also called the President a damned fool for issuing it. "Did
> Stanton say I was a damned fool?" asked Lincoln. "He did sir, and
> repeated it," replied the Congressman.

This accusation was no small thing. If true, it meant that a prominent cabinet member—the Secretary of War, no less—had just ignored his Commander in Chief's direct order and then compounded his offense by insulting the President of the United States in the presence of a sitting Congressman. By any military standard, Secretary Stanton was guilty of out-and-out mutiny. Lincoln's response reveals volumes about the man's character:

"If Stanton said I was a damned fool, then I must be one, for he is nearly always right, and generally says what he means. I will step over and see him." [143]

Personal feelings were subsumed to the vital interests of the nation.

This was humility and leadership at its best.

In 1838, Lincoln gave one of his first public addresses. It was to the Young Men's Lyceum of Springfield, Illinois. Lincoln was 28 years old. He had just moved to the town from a pioneer village. The incident that provoked the speech was the murder of a young black man in St. Louis, Missouri. He was burned to death by a mob. Lincoln spoke about the dangers of slavery and how it could corrupt the government and body politic. He told the story and what it meant:[144]

A mulatto man, by the name of McIntosh, was seized in the street, dragged to the suburbs of the city, chained to a tree, and actually burned to death; and all within a single hour from the time he had been a freeman, attending to his own business, and at peace with the world. Such are the effects of mob law.

Mob rule would mean mob justice, in Lincoln's view. The guilty and the innocent would be swept up in rage and irrationality. Even the members of the multitude that took justice in their own hands would not be spared. They, too, would be victims of the horde that tramples the law.

---

[143] Donovan Campbell, "The Leader's Code" (http://theleaderscode.com/excerpts/humility/)
[144] *Collected Works of Abraham Lincoln*, edited by Roy P. Basler et al. (http://www.abrahamlincolnonline.org/lincoln/speeches/lyceum.htm)

Lincoln was preaching for human rights and respect for the Bill of Rights, the Constitution, and the Declaration of Independence. Twenty-two years later, Lincoln would defend his fight to preserve the Union and end slavery, referring to basic principles of the American republic embodied in its sacred documents and history.

In the Lyceum speech, Lincoln revealed his sense of humility. He said every nation created "Napoleons" who had "towering ambition" and had a thirst to be famous. At the inception of the United States, one could be renowned by working to strengthen the young nation's institutions. Now those were in place, in Lincoln's view. "But now, success is assured. We are a success. And you do not get eternal fame by assuring the success of something that is already successful. You get it by changing the world."

Abraham Lincoln was ready to lead. He was not interested in glory. He wanted to right wrongs. He was humble but strong. He carried these qualities into the White House.

Lincoln liked people. He had a way where he could make the farmer, the artisan, and the banker feel at home. Most of his political enemies avoided meeting him. Once someone was in his presence, they felt a natural liking for Lincoln. It was a trait that he used to win over the opposition and to convince his Cabinet to his point of view.

1860 Political Cartoon, courtesy of National Archives

Lincoln was self-deprecating and modest, even about his responsibilities. He spoke about being "a humble instrument in the hands of the Almighty."[145] Lincoln managed to hold his temper even under the most stressful conditions. He responded to complaints, often in writing. He was straightforward but sensitive in his responses. He wrote: "Your words of kindness are incredibly grateful, but your suspicions that I intend you an injustice are very painful to me. I assure you such suspicions are groundless."[146]

Lincoln with his son Tad, courtesy of Library of Congress

---

[145] Michael Burlingame, editor, *Lincoln Observed: Civil War Dispatches of Noah Brooks*, p. 208 (from Noah Brooks, "Personal Recollections of Abraham Lincoln," *Harper's Monthly Magazine*, May 1865) (http://abraham-lincolnsclassroom.org/abraham-lincoln-in-depth/abraham-lincolns-personality/)
[146] Ibid. Burlingame

Lincoln concentrated on the point of view of others. He worked to repair hurt feelings, especially when it could escalate in permanent resentment. Lincoln gave credit easily, and took responsibility when things went badly. He credited Grant with defeating the South, for example, but admitted his own errors even when the failure was that of a subordinate. Lincoln was never provoked by petty situations. He was not jealous or held grudges.

Lincoln transformed his humility and human kindness into leadership strength. He combined it with self-confidence and sincere altruism. It became an essential quality of his mystique and the secret to his success. Lincoln showed that it takes greater effort and valor to be humble than to be egocentric.

Humble leaders are able to genuinely relate to and empathize with ordinary people. They do not consider themselves better or more important than others and they are able to easily acknowledge their own shortcomings and laugh at their blunders. Humble leaders realize they do not have all the answers, and they are willing to heed the advice and learn from the feedback of others.[147]

> At its essence, humility is nothing more than a realistic and unflinching view of yourself and your relationships. Humility is not self-deceit, self-denial, or self-flagellation. A leader grounds humility in an honest assessment of strengths and weaknesses, an inventory of the good, the bad, and the ugly. This self-understanding and self-reflection constitute humility. By gaining a deeper and more realistic knowledge of ourselves, we become humbler.

— Donovan Campbell

Humility may be the most difficult quality for leaders to express, yet it is among the most essential.

At times, it is mistaken for weakness.

---

[147] Dan Nielsen, *Presidential Leadership: Learning from United States*, Presidential Libraries & Museums (Dan Nielsen Company, 2013), p. 272

The gentle toughness of Lincoln combined with his ability to not take himself seriously made him a better and stronger leader who could know himself, as well as know others.

A humble Commander in Chief will know what they do not know and know how to compensate for it by taking action to find the best people to help him or her govern.

Lincoln Memorial, courtesy of National Archives

PART TWO: Leadership Qualities of The Commander in Chief
CHAPTER ELEVEN:
Passionate and Energetic

Every great dream begins with a dreamer. Always remember, you have within you the strength, the patience, and the passion to reach for the stars, to change the world.

— Harriet Tubman

Great ambition is the passion of a great character. Those endowed with it may perform very good or very bad acts. All depends on the principles which direct them.

— Napoleon Bonaparte

Passion is energy. Feel the power that comes from focusing on what excites you.

— Oprah Winfrey

We can each define ambition and progress for ourselves. The goal is to work toward a world where expectations are not set by the stereotypes that hold us back, but by our personal passion, talents, and interests.

— Sheryl Sandberg

Passion is one great force that unleashes creativity, because if you're passionate about something, then you're more willing to take risks.

— Yo-Yo Ma

Leadership is not about a title or a designation. It is about impact, influence, and inspiration. Impact involves getting results, influence is about spreading the passion you have for your work, and you have to inspire teammates and customers.

— Robin S. Sharma

Success comes to those who dedicate everything to their passion in life. To be successful, it is also very important to be humble and never let fame or money travel to your head.

— A. R. Rahman

Our most successful and memorable presidents led with passion and vigor. It was the love of the job, the desire to exercise the power and manage the levers of the presidency, and the desire to achieve, that made all the difference.

Within passion is energy.

Our most energetic leaders took on the duties with gusto. This love of life, this hunger to accomplish, and this high level of vitality concentrated on success is innate and not created. Few can learn to be 'passionate' about the presidency.

"The first thing that has to be recognized is that one cannot train someone to be passionate—it's either in their DNA or it's not," says Richard Branson, CEO of Virgin Airlines. "Believe me, I have tried and failed on more than one occasion, and it cannot be done, so don't waste your time and energy trying to light a fire under flame-resistant people."[148]

What distinguishes one passionate and energetic president from another is their approach to the presidency, their character, and how much they enjoy the job. How active they are is a clear sign. Active presidents often perform better. They lead with fervor and dynamism.

---

[148] Richard Branson, *The Virgin Way, Part Three, The Fruits of Passion,* Penguin: New York, 2014 (http://www.inc.com/richard-branson/passion-is-innate.html)

How briskly they approach problems and how much drive they devote to the task defines them as active vs. passive presidents. Close attention needs to be given to these qualities during campaigns to avoid putting into office the wrong person at the wrong time.

James David Barber devoted considerable attention to predicting performance in the White House.[149] Barber believed that the presidency was not just an institution, but a set of popular feelings embodied in the presidency. The Congress and the bureaucracy are often viewed as distinct and complex organizations by the public. In the presidency, people make sense of issues and where they rest their hopes and fears. It is the closest we get to an American monarchy.

Presidential Styles

The founding fathers left many things vague about the presidency. They knew that each new entrant would define the powers differently and distinctly. As a result, the office has evolved and changed based on the style and character of each occupant. Barber classified presidents into four categories, grounded on the activity or passivity that they brought to the position:

Active/Negative

These are gamblers who take risks. They do not like the political give and take and, as a result, rarely see the drawbacks of their decisions. Woodrow Wilson, Herbert Hoover, Lyndon Johnson, Richard Nixon, and George W. Bush fall into this category.

Active/Positive

These love the position. They pursue the duties aggressively. They strive for achievement and success, and they include Abraham Lincoln, Franklin Roosevelt, Theodore Roosevelt, Harry Truman, John Kennedy, Jimmy Carter. And recent observers have included Bill Clinton and Barack Obama.

---

[149] "Presidential Character and How to Foresee It," Chapter 1 of *The Presidential Character: Predicting Performance in the White House,* 4th ed., by James David Barber, pp. 1-1, 1, 493, Prentice Hall: New York, 1992

Passive/Positive

These are presidents who are often loved, but usually have few accomplishments. They search for affection as their reward and are cooperative and agreeable, rather than being assertive. Often, they project an image of optimism to dispel doubts and lift spirits to reduce the pain of politics. Presidents James Madison, William Howard Taft, Warren G. Harding, and Ronald Reagan are in this group, according to Barber.

Passive/Negative

These are the reluctant politicians who are in the position because they feel they need to be. They do not relish the responsibilities of the presidency, but they take them on as a duty to the nation. They are rarely innovators and work to keep stability. They are more laid back. George Washington is the classic case. He had to be persuaded to take on a second term. Calvin Coolidge and Dwight Eisenhower are other examples.

Candidates and presidents do not fall neatly into these groups. It is the tendency toward certain characteristics that need to be looked at. The key is to analyze the individual's personality before they get into the White House. By so doing, we can often predict, within limits, what they will be like in the Oval Office. An example of a passive/negative president is Theodore Roosevelt.

Colonel Theodore Roosevelt, courtesy of National Archives

Theodore Roosevelt: The First Modern President

Teddy Roosevelt was our first modern president. The presidency as we know it today, with its stature and influence, started with him. Edmund Morris described him this way:[150]

"They don't hold White House lunches the way they used to at the beginning of the century. On Jan. 1, 1907, for example, the guest list was as follows: a Nobel prizewinner, a physical culturalist, a naval historian, a biographer, an essayist, a paleontologist, a taxidermist, an ornithologist, a field naturalist, a conservationist, a big-game hunter, an editor, a critic, a ranchman, an orator, a country squire, a civil service reformer, a socialite, a patron of the arts, a colonel of the cavalry, a former governor of New York, the ranking expert on big-game mammals in North America, and the President of the U.S.

"All these men were named Theodore Roosevelt."

He was truly an American phenomenon. His passion, energy and vision were unique. No president before or after him had the same qualities. He read one to three books a day. During his presidency, he wrote 150,000 letters. Henry Adams said of him: "Power when wielded by abnormal energy is the most serious of facts .... Roosevelt, more than any other man living within the range of notoriety, showed the singular primitive quality that belongs to ultimate matter—he was pure Act."[151]

In the late 19th century, political parties and the Congress dominated the political scene. Through the force of his personality and aggressive executive action, Roosevelt changed the center of American politics to the Office of the President. He believed that the president should use all powers provided by the Constitution that were not specifically denied. He fought the notion of limited government action to right wrongs and correct social imbalances. He felt the president had a special relationship and responsibility to the people. Government was an agent of progress, reform, regulation, and conservation, and had the duty to make society fairer and more equitable, and share

---

[150] Edmund Morris, "Theodore Roosevelt," *Time* magazine, Monday, April 13, 1998
[151] Ibid. Morris

economic opportunities for all. He created five national parks, eighteen national monuments, and countless millions of trees in national forests, preserved for generations.

Before Roosevelt, big business was given a free hand to achieve their objectives. Teddy believed that big business had to be regulated and controlled in the public interest. He set out to break the large "trusts" and monopolies that dominated sectors of American business to make them more competitive.

He changed America's posture in global affairs. Roosevelt believed the United States had a global duty to protect its interests around the world.

Great White Fleet returning to Hampton Roads, December 1907, courtesy of Library of Congress

He vigorously pressed Congress to expand the Navy and launched the "Great White Fleet" to circle the earth and demonstrate American naval strength. The president wanted to exhibit expanding U.S. military power and oceanic naval capability. He wanted the fleet to also enforce treaties and protect sea lanes.

From a fleet of 90 small ships, many of them of wood, the fleet grew into a modern fighting force. The fleet of sixteen battleships, divided into two squadrons and various escorts, completed a circumnavigation of the globe from December 16, 1907, to February 22, 1909.

Photo # NH 106176-KN   Postcard welcoming U.S. fleet to Australia

Welcoming the Great White Fleet to Australia, 1908, courtesy of National Archives

The fleet was received in ports across the globe, as an example of American strength and American friendship.

President Theodore Roosevelt (on the 12-inch (30 cm) gun turret at right) addresses officers and crewmen on USS *Connecticut*, in Hampton Roads, Virginia, upon her return from the Fleet's cruise around the world, 22 February 1909, courtesy of Library of Congress

Roosevelt was determined to build the Panama Canal. He vigorously became involved in Latin American politics in order to do so. He ordered the building of the canal to start in 1903, after what he described as "three centuries of conversation." Teddy negotiated international peace treaties and worked to achieve a balance of power around the world.

1902 Political Cartoon of Teddy and the Trusts, courtesy of National Archives

Theodore Roosevelt introduced charisma to presidential politics. His strong rapport with the people and his way of working closely with the media helped shape public opinion. He continued his dynamic approach to policy issues even after he left office.

In 1912, The Progressive Party's New Nationalism platform echoed the liberal movements of the 1930's and 1960's that became the spirit of the New Deal, Harry Truman's Fair Deal, the New Frontier of John Kennedy, and the Great Society of Lyndon Johnson.

The presidency demands energy, good health, and resiliency. Theodore Roosevelt had it. It gave him the drive to approach the Office with passion and dedication.

Passion is energy. Feel the power that comes from focusing on what excites you.

— Oprah Winfrey

Enthusiasm is the yeast that makes your hopes shine to the stars. Enthusiasm is the sparkle in your eyes, the swing in your gait. The grip of your hand, the irresistible surge of will and energy to execute your ideas.

— Henry Ford

Success is almost totally dependent upon drive and persistence. The extra energy required to make another effort or try another approach is the secret of winning.

— Denis Waitley

The energy of the mind is the essence of life.

— Aristotle

PART TWO: Leadership Qualities of The Commander in Chief

CHAPTER TWELVE:

Flexible and Comfortable with Change

Great leaders are almost always great simplifiers, who can cut through argument, debate, and doubt to offer a solution everybody can understand.

— General Colin Powell

Defenders of the status quo will argue that this system has served us well over the centuries, that our parliamentary traditions have combined stability and flexibility, and that we should not cast away in a minute what has taken generations to build.

— Ferdinand Mount

Take advantage of the ambiguity in the world. Look at something and think what else it might be.

— Roger von Oech

On the road from the City of Skepticism, I had to pass through the Valley of Ambiguity.

— Adam Smith

It may be enough to study history in all its nuance and ambiguity for its own sake. But there is no country free of the need to find new ways of reading the past as an inspiring way of thinking about everything else, including the present.

— Colm Toibin

> *The battlefield is a scene of constant chaos. The winner will be the one who controls that chaos, both his own and the enemy's.*

> **— Napoleon Bonaparte**

> *To improve is to change; to be perfect is to change often.*

> **— Winston Churchill**

Each president and head of state deals with change.

Every era has ambiguities and each administration develops strategies to be flexible and cope with events.

Washington had the luxury of time. Information and transportation were slow, compared to today. But he and Lincoln were handicapped by the quality of data available and the speed at which they could receive and respond.

Today information is abundant and can be checked and double-checked immediately for accuracy.

Responses can be given instantaneously.

Twenty-first century leaders live in an era of the unexpected.

Things happen at lightning speed, due to technology.

The Commander in Chief must be resilient in the face of the unexpected. They must set the example to: [152]

- Demonstrate ability to deal with stress and pressure.
- Bounce back from setbacks and disappointments.
- Maintain optimism and a positive attitude in the face of new challenges and problems becoming ever more complex.
- Exhibit strong leadership even in the face of uncertainty.

---

[152] Melanie Allen, "Dealing with Ambiguity and Developing Resilience" (http://www.melanieallen.co.uk/articles/dealing-with-ambiguity/?utm_campaign=LinkedIn150&utm_content=Dealing%20with%20Ambiguity%20the%20New%20Business%20Imperative)

The personal qualities that presidents and their team bring to the job will determine how they handle the rapid evolution of events and challenges.

Dwight Eisenhower was a good example of this.

General Dwight Eisenhower, Supreme Allied Commander,
1945, courtesy of Library of Congress

Eisenhower and the National Security Council

Eisenhower was inaugurated as President in 1952. His predecessors, Harry Truman and Franklin Roosevelt, organized their White House in different ways. FDR often used his Brain Trust vs his Cabinet to make decisions. Truman relied on the Cabinet and his trusted experts and advisers to deal with ending World War II and dealing with the aftermath.

When Eisenhower came into office, the Soviet Union had the atomic bomb. They had occupied Eastern Europe and installed communist regimes. The Cold War had begun. The War in Korea needed to end. The post-World War II occupation of Europe and Japan required conclusion. The Marshall Plan for reconstruction of Europe was nearing completion. Domestic policies needed attention, like boosting employment and starting major infra-structure projects. Eisenhower was determined to simultaneously balance the budget and promote an era of peace and prosperity.

Eisenhower realized that the Cold War would be a long, drawn out effort to contain communism in the world and prevent the Soviet Union from expanding its imperialistic tendencies. He felt military means were not the full answer. Eisenhower had met and dealt with many Russian leaders during the War. He believed their main goal was survival in office and not world domination, even though they preached the spread of Marxism worldwide. He felt that the Soviet empire would evaporate from decay and its inability to deal with internal problems.

President Eisenhower's essential defense for the U.S. and its allies was to militarily fortify democracy and to help develop prosperity around the world. Containment of the Soviet Union demanded strengthening NATO and providing aid to developing countries to attain stability and democracy, and to reduce poverty.

Cold War Political Cartoon, courtesy of National Archives

He was concerned with the strategic cost involved with containing the global Soviet threat. No president after Eisenhower appreciated as much the financial risks of the Cold War. Failure to husband enough resources led directly to the costly dislocations and Cold War reversals of the 1970s and the massive deficits the nation still bears.[153]

President Eisenhower used his experience as a military leader to deal with the problems he faced when he came into office. He believed in careful staff work. Eisenhower preferred an organized chain of command that could quickly gather and analyze data and prepare responses for action.

"Ike" (he was elected on the slogan, "I like Ike") established administrative procedures for policy making and responses based on:[154]

- uncovering facts and careful examination to determine the truth
- options coordinated and approved by interested agencies, with disagreements highlighted and not compromised
- analysts ready to debate both sides of an issue in the presence of the president
- a final statement of the president's decision, to avoid uncertainty and ambiguity

President Truman created the National Security Council (NSC) in 1947, with the intent to ensure coordination among the military forces and the Central Intelligence Agency (CIA). He did that because he believed the State Department and diplomacy alone could not effectively deal with the Soviet threat.

Under Ike, the NSC evolved into the main arm of the president to implement international, military, and internal security policies. Eisenhower used the NSC extensively as his principle instrument to govern in a rapidly changing world that required immediate responses.

---

[153] Aaron Lobel, editor, "Presidential Judgment," *Futurecasts* online magazine, www.futurecasts.com, Volume 5, No. 1, 1/03
[154] Ibid. Lobel

The National Security Council consisted of the President, Vice President, Secretaries of State and Defense, and the Director of the Office of Defense Mobilization. A score of other Cabinet members and senior advisers could be called upon, depending on the question being dealt with. The Secretary of the Treasury and the Chairman of the Joint Chiefs of Staff often participated. The Director of Central Intelligence provided the NSC with regular briefings on global occurrences affecting national security.

The president gave special emphasis to the NSC meetings. He attended 173 of the 179 meeting during his first term. He missed six due to travel.

"At NSC meetings, Ike would actively question, comment, and sometimes play devil's advocate, to explore alternatives or the consequences or implications of some proposal. This system succeeded in producing active discussions and debates on contentious issues. Competing analyses and debate succeeded in facilitating informed and sound decisions."[155]

A major part of the NSC was the Planning Board (PB), which consisted of top-notch analysts who prepared policy reports that were reviewed at the meetings. The Board was responsible for creating "statesman-like-solutions" to thorny security problems. The PB presented candid views and searched for compromises among the other agencies.

Ike's approach to problem-solving and handling the unexpected was effective in keeping foreign crises from turning into military conflicts. It laid down a well-organized procedure for emergency preparedness and reduced risks in presidential decision-making. Ike cited several accomplishments as he left the White House in 1960:

- the national Interstate Highway system; St. Lawrence Seaway
- Civil Rights Bill of 1957
- balanced the Federal Budget
- ended the Korean War
- eight years of peace and economic growth

The Eisenhower approach was abandoned by John Kennedy and subsequent administrations.

The form of the NSC was maintained, but the substance of decision-making shifted to a handful of advisers, in most cases. The Assistant to the President for National Security became the key policy adviser to the Chief Executive. The NSC staff was large and seemed like a mini-Department of State. The Planning Board was eliminated.

As a result, presidential decisions became more "ad hoc," at the expense of long-term coherence and common sense. For example, the Bay of Pigs debacle might not have occurred if President Kennedy had used the NSC approach to analyze the details of the operation and anticipate the consequences of his decisions.[156]

LBJ's Great society by Lloyd Ostendorf,
courtesy of American Gallery—20th Century

---

[156] Ibid. Lobel

Lyndon Johnson used a personal approach to dealing with foreign policy and national security issues, often relying on his own instincts and experience in making judgments. He did not like large NSC meetings supported by extensive staff work. He, like Kennedy, was afraid of "leaks" of information reaching the media. Cabinet officers, like Dean Rusk and Robert McNamara, were reluctant to participate in sessions where extensive discussions were the norm and the chance that comments could reach the press were possible.

Richard Nixon relied on Henry Kissinger, his National Security Advisor, to plan and direct foreign policy from the Oval Office. The NSC under Kissinger was shaped to meet his needs and those of the president. The close relationship between Nixon and Kissinger led to dramatic foreign policy initiatives, like opening up diplomatically to China. Power increased for Kissinger, frequent consultations with President Nixon were held, and the authority of the NSC was unchallenged.

Gerald Ford kept Kissinger on when he took over from Nixon.

Jimmy Carter felt that the Kissinger/Nixon style of foreign policy was dangerous. Instead, he relied on his cabinet and left the NSC to be a policy arm of the Executive Branch.

A return to a more extensive use of the NSC came about during the administration of George H. W. Bush. He created a series of policy-coordinating committees that analyzed decisions for him in an organized manner. The new NSC stressed cooperation among the agencies and clear decision-making options for the president. The Bush changes were the closest to those originally put into place by Eisenhower.

Bill Clinton abolished the Bush procedure. He preferred a Presidential Decision Directive to promulgate executive decisions. He added a broad economic element to the work of the NSC. George W. Bush depended more on the Nixon/Kissinger model, with Condoleezza Rice as National Security Assistant, bolstered by Secretary of State Colin Powell and

Donald Rumsfeld at Defense. Like his immediate predecessors, President Obama used a small group of advisers to deal with foreign policy issues vs the full NSC process.[157]

The Commander in Chief should be measured by how he plans to face administratively the huge problems that are simultaneously happening around the world: economic decline, environmental challenges, terrorism, pandemics, and issues of war and peace.

Some thoughts, in this regard, in the era of the world wide web:[158]

- Not everything is controllable.
- Actions may have to be taken without complete knowledge, even though every effort should be made to make decisions based on all the known and knowable facts.
- Build a team of thinkers who anticipate the best and worst scenarios before they happen.
- Some choices will be wrong, but they may be better than no decision.
- Avoid decisions based on pride; if a bad decision was made, take responsibility, and make a new one.
- Be prepared for the unexpected.
- Plans need to be revisited and updated regularly.
- Show confidence by making thoughtful decisions and sticking to them.
- Listen carefully to everyone, even the critics.
- Be humble and avoid notoriety, even if you are the head of state.
- Most of all, be willing to give others credit when you succeed, and take the blame when you fail; this stimulates strong morale and loyalty, and promotes innovation.

---

[157] Karen DeYoung, "How the Obama Administration Runs Foreign Policy," *The Washington Post*, August 4, 2009
[158] Shaw, "Dealing with Ambiguity: The New Business Imperative," August 29, 2013 (https://www.linkedin.com/pulse/20130829124922-284615-dealing-with-ambiguity-the-new-business-imperative)

- Listen to your inner voice and intuition in making final decisions; you may not always be right, but you may not always be wrong, either.
- Surround yourself with the best and the brightest, and listen to them.
- Search for "contrarian views," and study them.
- Do not steal other's ideas, and try to give attribution where it is merited.
- Manage stress; the uncertainty in the world will overcome a leader who does not cultivate and maintain a relaxed state of mind.

Leadership is lonely. It requires mental and physical balance to maintain stability, particularly in the age of the Internet.

Lincoln relaxed by telling stories. At times, they were to make a point, but, more often, they allowed him to take his mind off the tragedies that encircled his daily life. He had a good sense of humor.

Illustrious leaders often do not take themselves seriously and are able to use humor to teach, as well as to reduce tension.

Responsibility results in high stress. It demands energy, careful pacing of work, and monitoring good health. Mental and physical health is essential, if a president is to tackle the obligations that come with command.[159]

Abraham Lincoln created the National Academy of Sciences in 1863. Since then, the scientific community has devoted itself to research and understanding the shape of things to come. Professor James Martin of the Oxford University Institute for Science and Civilization wrote *The Meaning of the 21st Century; A Vital Blueprint for Ensuring Our Future* (Riverhead, 2006).

---

[159] Ibid. Iodice, p. 282

In his study, he outlined these developments that will be part of the agenda dealing with change that the Commander in Chief of the United States — all leaders of democracies — will face:

- saving the earth
- reversing poverty
- steadying population growth
- achieving sustainable lifestyles
- preventing all-out war
- dealing effectively with globalism
- protecting the biosphere
- defusing terrorism
- conquering disease
- expanding human potential

PART TWO: Leadership Qualities of The Commander in Chief
CHAPTER THIRTEEN: ▬▬▬▬▬▬▬▬
Loves Learning

It's what you learn after you know it all, that counts.

— John Wooden

Live as if you were to die tomorrow. Learn as if you were to live forever.

— Mahatma Gandhi

Education is what remains after one has forgotten what one has learned in school.

— Albert Einstein

I am not afraid of storms, for I am learning how to sail my ship.

— Louisa May Alcott

I like to listen. I have learned a great deal from listening carefully. Most people never listen.

— Ernest Hemingway

You cannot open a book without learning something.

— Confucius

Being ignorant is not so much a shame as being unwilling to learn.

— Benjamin Franklin

We now accept the fact that learning is a lifelong process of keeping abreast of change. And the most pressing task is to teach people how to learn.

— Peter Drucker

A single conversation across the table with a wise man is better than ten years mere study of books.

— Henry Wadsworth Longfellow

In this life, you should read everything you can read. Taste everything you can taste. Meet everyone you can meet. Travel everywhere you can travel. Learn everything you can learn. Experience everything you can experience.

— Mario Cuomo

Writing — the art of communicating thoughts to the mind, through the eye — is the great invention of the world. Great in the astonishing range of analysis and combination ... great in enabling us to converse with the dead, the absent, and the unborn, at all distances of time and space.

— Abraham Lincoln

Lincoln at Antietam, courtesy of Library of Congress

Abraham Lincoln: Technology and Shakespeare

Learning is a key pillar of presidential leadership. Information is fast-paced and needs to be refreshed constantly. Talented leaders want facts, love knowledge, are curious about novelty, and appreciate that learning is a lifelong experience.

Great leaders learn from their peers. They meet and converse with others who are facing similar challenges.[160]

They pick up new ideas and have them analyzed. By reading, observing, questioning, and conversing, they are able to separate noises from signals, and comprehend trends and the shape of things to come.

Lincoln, for instance, was fascinated with creativity and innovations. He felt able to deal with challenges related to technology.

As a surveyor and patent lawyer, he was fascinated with inventions. Lincoln knew his lack of formal education limited his understanding of new discoveries, but it did not stop him from being eternally curious, especially about improvements that could change the outcome of the Civil War.

Any new firearm was of interest to him. He disliked hunting, but he was still proficient with a rifle and participated in marksmanship contests when visiting soldiers on the battlefield. Inventors of all sorts of weapons would descend on the White House to exhibit their "working models" to the president. If he were interested, he would turn them over to the professionals in the military to examine their feasibility.[161]

Lincoln read extensively.

He adored Shakespeare and recited passages from plays.

---

[160] Ibid. Iodice
[161] Robert Bruce, *Lincoln and the Tools of War*, University of Illinois Press: Springfield, 1989, p. 14

During a White House dinner with an actor as a guest, Lincoln said, "Some of Shakespeare's plays I have never read, while others I have gone over perhaps as frequently as any unprofessional reader. Among the latter are *Lear, Richard the Third, Henry the Eighth, Hamlet,* and especially *Macbeth.* I think nothing equals Macbeth."[162]

He enjoyed music and went to the theatre frequently. It was a way to relax from the rigors of his office.

Lincoln loved poetry. He memorized his favorite verses and recited them. He wrote several sonnets based on childhood memories. In the White House, he received from 50 to 250 letters a day, and some included poems. He read them with pleasure and saved some of them.[163] Poetry influenced his speaking and writing; Lincoln felt writing was the greatest idea man had ever created.

WORLD WAR II ALLIES - Russia's Joseph Stalin, FDR, and Winston Churchill of Great Britain meet in Teheran, Iran, November 29, 1943, courtesy of Roosevelt Library

[162] David Odegard, "The Favorite Books of All 44 Presidents of the United States," Feb. 17, 2014 (http://www.buzzfeed.com/daveodegard/the-favorite-books-of-all-44-presidents-of-the-united-states#.wbpn9bdpn)
[163] Fred Kaplan, *Lincoln: The Biography of a Writer* (HarperCollins: New York, as noted in the website of the Library of Congress, Lincoln and Poetry (http://www.loc.gov/rr/program/bib/lincolnpoetry/)

FDR: Avid Reader and Collector

Franklin Roosevelt was an avid reader with an interest in many subjects. His favorite authors were Kipling, Dickens, and Twain. He also read contemporary subjects, especially those related to history. He collected books, models of ships, and memorabilia of all sorts.

Scarcely a day would go by that FDR did not work on his stamp collection while in the White House. He found it linked him to history and geography around the world. His collection, at his death, had over 1,200,000 stamps. Those he received from foreign governments were donated to the Franklin Delano Roosevelt Presidential Library at Hyde Park.

He left to his Library 200 fully rigged ship models, 1,200 naval prints, and 15,000 books, thousands of pages of newspaper clippings, articles, speeches, letters, memos, and countless souvenirs of all sorts. FDR realized that to house his collection he would have to establish the first presidential library. He had the public interest in mind.

He wanted to create an historical research institution to educate the people about his time in office. On June 30, 1941, FDR opened the library with these words: [164]

The dedication of a library is in itself an act of faith. To bring together the records of the past and to house them in buildings where they will be preserved for the use of men and women in the future, a Nation must believe in three things. It must believe in the past. It must believe in the future. It must, above all, believe in the capacity of its own people so to learn from the past that they can gain in judgment in creating their own future.

---

[164] *Prologue Magazine*, National Archives, "Roosevelt and His Library," by Cynthia M. Koch and Lynn A. Bassanese, Summer 2001, Vol 33, No. 2

Much can be learned about a president or a candidate by what they read. Each of our presidents enjoyed reading before and during their time in the White House. What they read often showed what their priorities were and how they saw themselves as leaders, which may have affected the way they governed.

Certain books influenced their thinking and future policies.

Harry Truman read extensively about Andrew Jackson. He likened himself to "Old Hickory" in his plain origins, and to his direct style of speaking and governing.[165]

A book review influenced John Kennedy to launch a major policy initiative of his administration. After reading about Michael Harrington's *The Other America*, which was about poverty, he asked his staff to look into the issue and come up with an "attack on poverty." This was shortly before his trip to Dallas, in November 1963.[166]

Barbara Ward's, *Rich Nations and Poor Nations*, influenced Lyndon Johnson, Kennedy's successor. He read the British author's book several times. It inspired him to move ahead with the War on Poverty and to realize Kennedy's vision.

Richard Nixon was an avid reader of Tolstoy. He also read books about the major issues of the day. After meeting with the Soviets, for example, he read Churchill's *Triumph and Tragedy*, which chronicled Churchill's experience at the Yalta Conference in 1945.

Edmund Morris' books on Theodore Roosevelt were among Ronald Reagan's favorites. Morris, in fact, became Reagan's official biographer. *The Gipper* was the first of several books on a president to highlight

---

[165] Jon Meacham, "How to Read Like a President," New York Times Essay, October 31, 2008 (http://www.nytimes.com/2008/11/02/books/review/Meacham-t.html?_r=0)

[166] Tevi Troy, "For Obama and past presidents, the books they read shape policies and perceptions," *The Washington Post*, Sunday, April 18, 2010

works of conservative economists and intellectuals like *Free to Choose*, by Milton Friedman, and George Gilder's *Wealth and Poverty*.[167]

Ralph Ellison, Maya Angelou, and Taylor Branch were among Bill Clinton's favorite writers. He loved mysteries. He often stressed books of thinkers, like Yale law professor Stephen Carter, by displaying them prominently in the Oval Office. *The Balkan Ghosts* by Robert Kaplan apparently influenced Clinton's decision to intervene in Bosnia.

During his second term, George W. Bush read extensively. He liked what were described as "prescriptive books" like *Supreme Command* by Eliot A. Cohen and *The Case for Democracy* by Natan Sharansky. These advocated military and nation-building policies. Bush met with authors whose books he enjoyed. Sharansky, for example, spent an hour with him in the Oval Office discussing how to advance democracy in the world. "Not only did he read it," said Sharansky, "he felt it."[168]

Free nations need leaders who love learning and understand the importance of education for their country.

Sometimes, an effort comparable to landing a man on the moon is needed to revitalize a nation's educational systems.

Tony Wagner, in his book, *The Global Achievement Gap*, outlined what is essential for learning in the 21st Century:

- critical thinking and problem solving
- collaboration across networks and leading by influence
- agility and adaptability
- initiative and entrepreneurialism
- effective oral and written communication
- accessing and analyzing information

---

[167] Ibid. Troy
[168] Ibid. Troy

- curiosity and imagination

The Commander in Chief of every country should be that country's top educator. They all must emphasize learning at all levels if mankind is to survive and thrive on this planet.

PART TWO: Leadership Qualities of The Commander in Chief
CHAPTER FOURTEEN:
Respects Diversity

Tolerance implies no lack of commitment to one's own beliefs. Rather it condemns the oppression or persecution of others.

— John F. Kennedy

What is tolerance? It is the consequence of humanity. We are all formed of frailty and error; let us pardon reciprocally each other's folly — that is the first law of nature.

— Voltaire

The highest result of education is tolerance.

— Helen Keller

Tolerance is giving to every other human being every right that you claim for yourself.

— Robert Gree

The responsibility of tolerance lies with those who have the wider vision.

— George Eliott

It is not how much or how little you have that makes you great or small, but how much or how little you are with what you have.

— Rabbi Samson Raphael Hirsch

> *Intolerance lies at the core of evil. Not the intolerance that results from any threat or danger. But intolerance of another being who dares to exist. Intolerance without cause. It is so deep within us, because every human being secretly desires the entire universe to himself. Our only way out is to learn compassion without cause. To care for each other simply because that 'other' exists.*

— Rabbi Menachem Mendle

Lincoln and the Jews

The United States is, by far, one of the most diverse cultures in the world.

Every race, creed, and color are in America. Our strength is our diversity. Our president must see it this way. Our power as a people is the respect for our differences. It was not always such, especially when we recall our experience with slavery, the rights of women, religious discrimination, and intolerance toward those unlike ourselves. Immigrants faced this challenge from the beginnings of our republic.

One of our presidents was the glowing example of how we should be and how every president should be when it comes to treating other human beings.

He followed the Golden Rule.

He was tolerant, understanding of the rights of minorities and those without the power to defend themselves. He lived his life like he preached it and professed it.

His name was Abraham Lincoln.

The last posed photograph of Abraham Lincoln, taken ten weeks
before his assassination by Alexander Gardner, courtesy of Library of Congress

We know so much about him and the plight of African Americans and his rejection of slavery, but there is another example that today gives us an additional dimension to Lincoln that we did not know before.

His relationship with Jews was an illustration of his good heart, his sense of fairness, and his desire to allow all Americans a chance to live peacefully in their chosen land without the heavy hand of prejudice oppressing them.[169]

From his earliest days in Kentucky and Illinois, Lincoln had met Jews.

One of his closest associates and friends was Abraham Jonas. He was a lawyer, born in England, who had come to the U.S. in 1819. Jonas and Lincoln were supporters of Henry Clay and the Whigs. Jonas helped organize the Lincoln and Douglas debates and worked to help him become President. Lincoln made him a postmaster in Quincy, Illinois.

---

[169] "The Unusual Relationship Between Abraham Lincoln and the Jews" (http://mosaicmagazine.com/observation/2015/04/the-unusual-relationship-between-abraham-lincoln-and-the-jews/)

Shortly after Jonas's death, Lincoln appointed his widow to the post in order not to leave the family without a livelihood. Lincoln was close to Jonas' children. Five of them moved to the South.

Two joined the Confederate cause.

Even so, Lincoln's relationship with them was considerate and compassionate. One of Jonas's sons, an attorney, asked Lincoln in 1857 to help release a black man imprisoned in New Orleans because he lacked papers. Lincoln moved swiftly. He secured the money to save the man. In the middle of the Civil War, Lincoln's friend, Abraham Jonas, was dying. The president allowed one of Jonas's sons, a Confederate prisoner of war, a parole to see his father before he died.

The Jonas friendship is only one example of Lincoln's respect and admiration for Jews. More important, Lincoln wanted to promote a sense of fairness toward them and other minorities.

He arranged for Jews to be appointed to positions in the War effort. He overturned an edict from his most popular General, Ulysses S. Grant, expelling Jewish merchants who were suspected of selling contraband. Lincoln would not accept such an edict, which was clearly without merit.

Abraham Lincoln ran countercurrent to the thinking of his day.

His approach to Jews is a case point of his broadmindedness and acceptance of all those who faced subjugation and persecution and who were misjudged and mistreated just because they were in the minority.

His magnificent qualities of kindness, empathy, and open-mindedness were demonstrated by actions throughout his life and during his time as Chief Executive of the United States.

Lincoln showed us what a president of the United States must have to be the leader of not just some of the people, but of *all* of the people.

PART TWO: Leadership Qualities of The Commander in Chief
CHAPTER FIVETEEN: ━━━━━━━
Trust

It takes 20 years to build a reputation, and five minutes to ruin it.

— Warren Buffett

Whoever is careless with the truth in small matters cannot be trusted with important matters.

— Albert Einstein

I have no fear that the result of our experiment will be that men may be trusted to govern themselves without a master.

— Thomas Jefferson

Trust, but verify.

— Ronald Reagan

Responsibilities are given to him on whom trust rests. Responsibility is always a sign of trust.

— James Cash Penne

He who does not trust enough, will not be trusted.

— Lao Tzu

I cannot trust a man to control others who cannot control himself.

— Robert E. Lee

Trust has to be earned, and should come only after the passage of time.

— Arthur Ashe

Few things can help an individual more than to place responsibility on him, and to let him know that you trust him.

— B. T. Washington

Government is a trust, and the officers of the government are trustees. And both the trust and the trustees are created for the benefit of the people.

— Henry Clay

The Vietnam War

Vietnam: Confusing, oxymoronic, lethal, torrential, steaming, wasteful . . . . They came home without leaving Vietnam, angry and depressed, retreating from the world and burdened by memories of the dead . . . the war taught a generation of young people not to trust their government.

— Stars and Stripes

Vietnam Memorial, Washington, D.C., courtesy of National Archives

By the time U.S. military involvement in Vietnam ended in August 1975, 282,000 Allied military personnel had died. 58,220 were Americans. And 444,000 North Vietnamese and Viet Cong lost their lives, along with 587,000 North and South Vietnamese civilians. In all, 1,313,000 people died in the War in Vietnam. Nearly 3 million Americans served in Vietnam. . .10% of their generation.[170]

Americans fought bravely. They won nearly every battle and were awarded 250 Medals of Honor.

But it was all in vain.

"They, and so many others who fought in Vietnam, were as great as any generation that preceded them. Their misfortune was to draw a bad war, an unnecessary war, a mistake by American politicians and statesmen, for which they paid."[171]

---

[170] Lewy, Guenter (1978), *America in Vietnam*, Oxford University Press: New York, pp. 442–453

[171] Neil Sheehan, "At the Bloody Dawn of the Vietnam War," *The New York Times*, November 13, 2015

Many returned home disillusioned with the government that sent them to fight in a far-off jungle for a questionable cause. Millions of Americans protested the war across the United States for nearly a decade. Americans and many of their leaders lost faith in their government. "The biggest lesson I learned from Vietnam is not to trust our own government statements. I had no idea until then that you could not rely on them," former Sen. J. William Fulbright.[172]

Hundreds of thousands of bombs, and tens of thousands of gallons of Agent Orange, were dropped on Vietnam. Nearly fifty years after the end of the war, the Vietnamese are still cleaning up the land ravaged by one of the fiercest bombing campaigns in history. The U.S. government is paying for part of the effort[173]

What can never be repaid is the human suffering caused by the Vietnam War and the loss of faith in our political system and way of life. Vietnam was caused by presidential leadership, and presidential decisions, that were wrong, and lies and mistruths that created a lasting sense of mistrust toward our system of government, which prevails to the present day.

Secretary of Defense Robert McNamara served John Kennedy and Lyndon Johnson. He was a chief architect of the war. In his book, *Retrospect: The Tragedy and Lessons of Vietnam*, he said:[174]

> *Although we sought to do the right thing — and believed we were doing the right thing — in my judgment, hindsight proves us wrong. We both overestimated the effects of South Vietnam's loss on the security of the West and failed to adhere to the fundamental principle that, in the final analysis, if the South Vietnamese were to be saved, they had to win the war themselves.*

---

[172] Terry Leonard, "Vietnam at 50," *Stars and Stripes*, 2015 (http://www.stripes.com/news/special-reports/vietnam-at-50)

[173] George Black, "The Lethal Legacy of the Vietnam War," Fifty years after the first US troops came ashore at Da Nang, the Vietnamese are still coping with unexploded bombs and Agent Orange. *The Nation*, February 25, 2015 (http://www.thenation.com/article/lethal-legacy-vietnam-war/)

[174] "Legacy of the Vietnam War" (http://www.footprinttravelguides.com/asia/vietnam/about-vietnam/legacy-of-the-vietnam-war/;) *Retrospect, The Tragedy of the Vietnam War,* Robert McNamara, Vintage Books: New York, March 1998

Presidential Historian Doris Kearns Goodwin commented on the legacy of the Vietnam War and presidential leadership:[175]

> *The most important lesson that people have to take from the war ... is that no foreign war can succeed without that large domestic support. Franklin Roosevelt understood that way back in the 30's when he gave the "Quarantine the Aggressor" speech, and the country didn't respond to want to go get involved in Europe's war. Later, he said it is like looking back in a parade and no one's following you. You cannot go forward. So wherever we lay blame or not, I think there's no question that the lesson to be learned is you have to level with the country, you have to make them understand the price they're paying.*

While the Vietnam War was continuing during Richard Nixon's second term, another incident happened that shook the trust of the American people in their government and the presidency: Watergate.

The Watergate Scandal

> *The impact is deep and will be enduring. It will be a long time, if ever, before politics in the United States is the same again.*

> **— U.S. News and World Report, August 8, 2014**

Senate Watergate Committee holding a press conference,
courtesy of US Senate Historical Office

---

[175] Doris Kearns Goodwin, "PBS News Hour, Vietnam's Legacy," April 5, 2000 (http://www.pbs.org/newshour/bb/asia-jan-june00-vietnam_4-5/TOPICS > Nation)

After Gerald Ford pardoned Richard Nixon in September 1974, Nixon expressed regret and released this statement: [176]

I was wrong in not acting more decisively and more forthrightly in dealing with Watergate, particularly when it reached the stage of judicial proceedings and grew from a political scandal into a national tragedy. No words can describe the depth of my regret and pain at the anguish my mistakes over Watergate have caused the nation and the presidency, a nation I so deeply love, and an institution I so greatly respect.

Watergate overshadowed the Nixon presidency. Many Americans remember him as the first president to resign from office, not for his achievements. The affair left such a lasting impression around the world that many scandals since then have been labeled with the suffix, "gate."

The scandal resulted in a chain reaction of measures to reign in presidential power. A series of laws were passed reducing the president's ability to wage undeclared war, strengthening public access to government information, and curbs on campaign spending. The Freedom of Information Act was amended. New financial disclosure policies went into effect for top government officials.

The incident proved that the Constitutional system of checks and balances works.

---

[176] "The Effects of Watergate," Boundless U.S. History; Boundless, 21 Jul. 2015, retrieved 13 October 2015 (https://www.boundless.com/u-s-history/textbooks/boundless-u-s-history-textbook/the-conservative-turn-of-america-1968-1989)

1974 Political Cartoon depicting Watergate's damage
to the Presidency, courtesy of National Archives

By far the most significant impact was the public's loss of trust in the presidency, elected officials, politicians, and government in general. Cynicism and skepticism concerning the character, honesty, and motives of elected officials would be broad, deep, and long lasting.[177]

Karl Hubenthal, 1975, courtesy of Ohio State University Cartoon Research Library

[177] Ibid. Boundless

The political fallout for Republicans was almost immediate: Democrats made significant gains in the 1974 midterm elections and took the White House in 1976.

Almost half a century after Vietnam and Watergate, Americans are still skeptical about the government.

The Commander in Chief is responsible for building and keeping trust with the people.

A good example of a leader who was able to capture and maintain the trust of the people was Franklin Delano Roosevelt. He did it by acting, communicating, and staying close to the people and their institutions. He made it a point to reach into the households of ordinary Americans and speak to them, calm their fears, and give them hope. It was this hope that ultimately carried the nation through hard times and helped us win World War II.

FDR: Gaining the Public Trust

Franklin Roosevelt used the radio, the media, and the pen to talk with the people. He received letters throughout his presidency and responded personally, when possible.

President Franklin D. Roosevelt received an average of 8,000 letters, cards, and telegrams daily.
Courtesy of Franklin D. Roosevelt Presidential Library

His Fireside Chats via the radio generated an unprecedented tide of mail. On average, a broadcast would generate 450,000 letters, telegrams, and cards. Herbert Hoover, FDR's predecessor, received about 800 letters a day. Roosevelt received more than 8000.

What follows are a few letters from the Franklin D. Roosevelt Presidential Library that he received, which show the impact he had on the public with his Fireside Chats: [178]

OCTOBER 1, 1934

Dear Mr. President,

Everybody who has any sense and was able to get to a radio heard your speech last night. I desire to add my firm approval to every utterance which came from your lips.

Surely under the guidance of your great constructive genius the country is gaining. It is well that you take us into your confidence and tell us, Mr. President; your address reveals what we had not heard. There is such a welter of publicity about the alphabetized programs that much wisdom is lost in confusion, but when you speak, everybody understands.

You know what your government is doing. You know how to explain it. You know where you are heading, and you are on your way. God bless and keep you strong for the battle, Mr. President, is the sincere wish of a red-hot, jet-black Democrat.

Melvin J. Chisum
(Field Secretary of the National Negro Press Association)

Philadelphia, Pa.

---

[178] American Radio Works, "Letters to Franklin Delano Roosevelt," November 10, 2014 (http://www.americanradioworks.org/segments/letters-to-franklin-delano-roosevelt/)

APRIL 28, 1942

Dear Frank:

And I use this salutation respectfully, warmly. For any man who could come so close to people of the U.S. as you did tonight, certainly knows them well enough to be called by his first name.

This is from a 26 1/2-year-old chemical engineer who would almost rather die than write a letter . . . .

Frank, tonight you made me proud of being an American and you made me want to write, made the urge to do so irresistible . . . .

Frank, there is one thrill, one sublime thrill that you will never know, or, rather, experience. And that is the thrill that comes to a person – who, having been brought up in a poor family, experienced and felt keenly many of the injustices in our system – when he hears one of our leaders, – – who has every justifiable right and reason, judging from his background, to be perfectly unaware of these inequalities – dedicate himself and rededicate the nation to the sublime principles of true democracy.

You see, Frank, there were times when my head was heavy and filled with doubts, times such as the miserable shooting on the bonus army, or times, when as a relief investigator I visited hundreds of downtrodden and almost hopeless families, or events such as the Republic Steel massacre in Chicago – and I wondered whether democracy would ever rise above such low levels.

Tonight, you reaffirmed my faith and reawakened in me, that which I thought was no longer there, namely, a feeling of being one of a large, united family, and a hope that this family, – Christian and Jew, White, Yellow and Black – could and would live and work harmoniously together until victory is won – and forever after. – Tonight, you gave me that thrill. And for that I am deeply grateful . . . .

Thank you fervently.

Your friend,

Joseph J. Hitov

DECEMBER 24, 1943

Dear Mr. President –

You have just finished speaking over the radio. Until you spoke, I had been dreading Christmas Eve a little. My husband, Captain Allen Schauffler, is with A.W.G. attached to the British Eighth Army in Italy, and my young son is in the Amphibious Command. But I want you to know that what you have just said so simply and honestly, has made everything seem right – and I am not dreading Christmas any longer. As you spoke it seemed as if Allen were sitting here beside me, listening with me, as we have listened to you together so many times.

Thank you, from the bottom of my heart.

Gratefully yours,

Helen Powell Schauffler New Rochelle, N.Y.

Franklin Delano Roosevelt died in Warm Springs, Georgia, on April 12, 1945. His body was brought to Washington, D.C. to lie in state, and then to be taken to the home of FDR in Hyde Park, New York, to be laid to rest.

The funeral procession passed the White House. A reporter saw a young man in uniform standing outside of the gates of the Presidential Mansion, crying profusely.

"Did you know the President?" asked the reporter. "No sir, I didn't know Roosevelt . . . but Roosevelt knew me."[179]

---

[179] FDR, "A Presidency Revealed," The History Channel, historychannel.com, 2000

CONCLUSION ━━━━━━━━━━━━━━━━━━━━

A leader who holds the destiny of a nation in their hands should be an "idealist without illusions."

Leadership must be realistic, wise, humble, and qualified.

Those who take on the burden of responsibility, as guides of their people through times of peace and peril, must be trustworthy, as well as competent.

Without trust, there is no leadership.

No one person possesses all the necessary qualities of a country's Commander in Chief, as examined in this work.

Those traits have been applied in history, with many a success and many a failure.

We, as citizens of a free nation, are obliged to insist that those who want to command have the characteristics of our greatest leaders.

When we accept less, we put our lives, our fortunes, and our future in danger.

BIBLIOGRAPHY ━━━━━━━━━━━━━━━━━━

Lincoln Biographies

Beveridge, Albert J. *Abraham Lincoln: 1809-1858* (1928). 2 vols. Online edition.

Burlingame, Michael. *Abraham Lincoln: A Life*. 2 vols. 2008).

Carwardine, Richard. *Lincoln: A Life of Purpose and Power*. 2003.

Cuomo, Mario. *Why Lincoln Matters*. Harcourt: New York. 2004.

DeRose, Chris. *Congressman Lincoln: The Making of America's Greatest President*. http://www.amazon.com/Congressman-Lincoln-Chris-DeRose/dp/1451695144. 2013.

Gienapp, *William E. Abraham Lincoln and Civil War America: A Biography*. Online edition. 2002.

Goodwin, Doris Kearns. *Team of Rivals: The Political Genius of Abraham Lincoln*. 2005.

Guelzo, Allen C. *Abraham Lincoln: Redeemer President*. Online edition. 1999.

Harris, William C. *Lincoln's Rise to the Presidency*. 2007.

Nicolay, John George, and John Hay. *Abraham Lincoln: A History*. 1890. online at Volume 1 and Volume 2 and Vol 6; 10 volumes in all.

Neely, Mark E. *The Last Best Hope of Earth: Abraham Lincoln and the Promise of America.* 1993.

Oates, Stephen B. W*ith Malice Toward None: The Life of Abraham Lincoln.* 1994. excerpt and text search.

Sandburg, Carl. *Abraham Lincoln: The Prairie Years.* 2 Vols. 1926. *The War Years.* 4 Vols, 1939. Vol V, 2 online.

Thomas, Benjamin P. *Abraham Lincoln: A Biography.* 1952; 2nd ed., 2008. online edition.

White, Ronald C. Jr. *A. Lincoln: A Biography.* Random House: New York, 2009.

White, Ronald C. Jr. *The Eloquent President.* Random House: 2005.

White, Ronald C. Jr., *Lincoln's Greatest Speech.* Simon and Shuster: New York, 2002.

Presidential Biographies

Bumiller, Elisabeth (January 2009). "Inside the Presidency." *National Geographic,* (1): 130–149. 2015.

Beschloss, Michael. *Presidential Courage: Brave Leaders and How They Changed America,* 1789-1989. Simon & Schuster. May 2000.

Couch, Ernie. *Presidential Trivia.* Rutledge Hill Press. March 1, 1996.

Lang, J. Stephen. *The Complete Book of Presidential Trivia.* Pelican Publishing. 2001.

Leo, Leonard, James Taranto, and William J. Bennett. *Presidential Leadership: Rating the Best and the Worst in the White House.* Simon and Schuster: 2004.

Presidential Studies Quarterly. Published by Blackwell Synergy, a quarterly academic journal on the presidency.

Waldman, Michael, and George Stephanopoulos. *My Fellow Americans: The Most Important Speeches of America's Presidents, from George Washington to George W. Bush.* Sourcebooks Trade: 2003. ISBN: 1-4022-0027-7.

Winder, Michael K. *Presidents and Prophets: The Story of America's Presidents and the LDS Church.* Covenant Communications. 2007.

Presidential Histories

Jacobs, Ron. Interview with Joseph G. Peschek and William Grover, authors of *The Unsustainable Presidency.*

"A New Nation Votes: American Election Returns, 1787–1825." Presidential election returns, including town and county breakdowns. https://login.ezproxy.library.tufts.edu/login?auth=tufts&url=http://elections.lib.tufts.edu/.

"The American Presidency Project". UC Santa Barbara. Retrieved October 7, 2005. Collection of over 67,000 presidential documents.

The History Channel: U.S. Presidents

"All the President's Roles." Ask Gleaves. Hauenstein Center for Presidential Studies, Educational site on the American Presidency. Retrieve3d October 20, 2006.

"Presidents' Occupations." Retrieved August 20, 2007.

"The Presidents." American Experience. PBS site on the American Presidency. Retrieved March 4, 2007.

Presidents of the United States: Resource Guides from the Library of Congress: Franklin Delano Roosevelt Biographies

Davis, Kenneth S. *FDR: The Beckoning of Destiny,* 1882–1928. Popular biography. ISBN: 978-0-399-10998-0. 1972.

Freidel, Frank (1952–73). *Franklin D. Roosevelt.* 4 volumes. *Franklin D. Roosevelt: A Rendezvous with Destiny* (scholarly biography). One volume, covers entire life. 1990.

Goodwin, Doris Kearns. *No Ordinary Time: Franklin and Eleanor Roosevelt: The Home Front in World War II.* 1995.

Gunther, John. *Roosevelt in Retrospect.* Harper & Brothers. 1950.

Hawley, Ellis. *The New Deal and the Problem of Monopoly.* Fordham University Press. ISBN: 0-8232-1609-8. 1995.

Jenkins, Roy. *Franklin Delano Roosevelt.* Short bio from British perspective. ISBN: 978-0-8050-6959-4. 2003.

Lash, Joseph P. *Eleanor and Franklin: The Story of Their Relationship Based on Eleanor Roosevelt's Private Papers.* History of a marriage. 1971.

Pederson, William D. *A Companion to Franklin D. Roosevelt, Companions to American History.* Blackwell. 35 essays by scholars. 2011.

Rowley, Hazel. *Franklin and Eleanor: An Extraordinary Marriage.* Farrar, Straus & Giroux. 2010.

Siracusa, Joseph M., and David G. Coleman. *Depression to Cold War: A History of America from Herbert Hoover to Ronald Reagan.* Greenwood Publishing. 2002.

Smith, Jean Edward. *FDR.* New York: Random House. 2007.

Tully, Grace. *Franklin Delano Roosevelt, My Boss.* Kessinger Publishing. 2005.

Winkler, Allan M. *Franklin D. Roosevelt and the Making of Modern America.* Longman. 2006.

Other Sources

Franklin D. Roosevelt Presidential Library and Museum.

Franklin Delano Roosevelt Memorial, Washington, DC.

Full text and audio of a number of Roosevelt's speeches – Miller Center of Public Affairs.

Franklin Delano Roosevelt: A Resource Guide from the Library of Congress.

Bibliography

ABOUT THE AUTHOR

Emilio Iodice

Director Emeritus, Professor of Leadership, Loyola University Chicago
John Felice Rome Center
Former Executive and U.S. Diplomat
Award Winning Writer, Historian, Public Speaker

Emilio Iodice was born in the South Bronx in 1946. He was the son of immigrants from the island of Ponza in Italy. He grew up in a truly bi-cultural environment: living in Little Italy and America at the same time. He worked full time while studying to pay for his education, from elementary school to graduate school, and still managed to complete his studies at the top of his class.

Iodice received his BS in Business from Fordham University, his MBA from the Bernard Baruch School of the City University of New York, and was named to BETA GAMMA SIGMA, the honorary society of distinguished graduates in Business. He conducted doctoral work in International Business and Applied Finance at George Washington University in Washington, DC.

Iodice spent over four decades as a senior executive in the public and private sectors, as an educator, and as a university administrator. Those forty years of experience included being a key official in Washington, DC, working for several administrations, and reaching the top ranks of the Civil Service and the Diplomatic Corps.

He was among the most decorated officers in American history, with a Gold Medal for Heroism, a Gold Medal and Silver Medal for Exemplary Service, nominations for the Bronze Medal, and numerous commendations and citations. He served as Minister in key U.S. missions abroad, including Brasilia, Mexico City, Rome, Madrid, and Paris, and departed after being named to the list of future Ambassadors.

Among his honors were being Knighted by the former King of Italy, and also named an honorary Guard of the Pantheon for the Royal Family. He received Medals of Honor from Spain and Italy. At age 33, he was named by the President of the United States to the prestigious Senior Executive Service as a Charter Member. He was the youngest career public official to reach this distinction.

Before joining Loyola, he was Vice President of Lucent Technologies in charge of operations in numerous countries, and later taught full time as an Assistant Professor at Trinity College in Washington, DC. He joined Loyola in 2007 as Director of the John Felice Rome Center. After one year he was promoted to Vice President. After serving for nine years as Vice President and Director, he was awarded the title of Director Emeritus and Professor of Leadership on June 30, 2016.

He speaks several languages and has traveled across the globe. His passions in life have been writing and educating others; assisting those in need; the Loyola Rome Center, its students, faculty, and staff; good music; reading; his family and, in particular, his four grandchildren and god children. His academic field of study was "Leadership."

He wrote and published numerous peer-reviewed articles on leadership in the *Journal of Values Based Leadership* of Valparaiso University in Indiana, which have been read across the globe. He was also a member of the Editorial Board of the Journal and is a member of the Board of Regents of Marymount International in Rome, Italy, and Istituto Marymount.

In 2012, his bestselling book on tenor Mario Lanza was published, entitled, *A Kid from Philadelphia, Mario Lanza: The Voice of the Poets.* In 2013 his second book, *Profiles in Leadership: From Caesar to Modern Times,* was published by North American Business Press along with *Sisters,* the story of two extraordinary people, his mother and his aunt. In 2014, he published *Future Shock 2.0, The Dragon Brief 2020,* and *Reflections, Stories of Love, Leadership, Courage and Passion.* In 2016 he launched, *2016, Selecting the President, The Most Important Decision You Will Ever Make.* In 2017, his new book was published: *When Courage was the Essence of Leadership, Lessons from History,* which reached number one bestseller status in the world in the field of leadership. *Profiles in Leadership: From Caesar to Modern Times* and *Reflections* were translated into Italian and published in 2017 and immediately reached bestseller status.

His works can be found on this Amazon site: https://www.amazon.com/Emilio-Iodice/e/B00HR6PNFW/ref=dbs_p_pbk_rwt_abau

In March 2019, the Iodice Leadership Center was established in St. Barnabas High School in the Bronx, to train young female students in the art and science of leadership.

ISBN: No. 1-2795555391

INDEX

Courtesy of Mount Rushmore National Memorial